sugar & spice

sugar & spice

a book of sweet delights

emma **summer**

southwater

This edition is published by Southwater
Southwater is an imprint of Anness Publishing Ltd

Hermes House, 88–89 Blackfriars Road, London SE1 8HA
tel. 020 7401 2077; fax 020 7633 9499

info@anness.com

© Anness Publishing Ltd 1999, 2002

Published in the USA by Southwater, Anness Publishing Inc.
27 West 20th Street, New York, NY 10011;
fax 212 807 6813

This edition distributed in the UK by
The Manning Partnership
251–253 London Road East, Batheaston,
Bath BA1 7RL

This edition distributed in the USA by
National Book Network
4720 Boston Way, Lanham, MD 20706

This edition distributed in Canada by General Publishing
895 Don Mills Road, 400–402 Park Centre, Toronto, Ontario
M3C 1W3

This edition distributed in Australia by
Sandstone Publishing
Unit 1, 360 Norton Street, Leichhardt,
New South Wales 2040

This edition distributed in New Zealand by
The Five Mile Press (NZ) Ltd
PO Box 33-1071 Takapuna, Unit 11/101-111
Diana Drive, Glenfield, Auckland 10

A CIP catalogue record for this book is available from the
British Library.

Publisher Joanna Lorenz
Executive Editor Linda Fraser
Project Editors Sarah Ainley, Emma Brown and Emma Clegg
Designers Patrick McLeavey & Partners
Illustrator Anna Koska
Photographers Karl Adamson, Edward Allwright, Steve Baxter,
James Duncan, Michelle Garrett,
Amanda Heywood, Don Last and Thomas Odulate
Recipes Carla Capalbo, Jacqueline Clark,
Carole Clements, Joanna Farrow, Rafi Fernandez, Christine
France, Sarah Gates, Shirley Gill,
Ruby Le Bois, Laura Washburn, Stephen Wheeler
and Elizabeth Wolf-Cohen
Reader Diane Ashmore
Production Controller Wendy Lawson

Previously published in two separate volumes *The Little Dessert
Cookbook* and *The Little Ice Cream Cookbook*.

10 9 8 7 6 5 4 3 2 1

Notes
Standard spoon and cup measures are level.

Large eggs are used unless otherwise stated.

Contents

Introduction

The strong-willed reach resolutely for the fruit bowl at the conclusion of every meal, but most of us would much rather be treated to a luxurious, magical, spirit-lifting dessert. Cool and creamy, sweet and fruity, or simply drowning in chocolate, desserts are destined to remain on the menu. Whatever the season, there's a perfect sweet delight waiting in the wings, whether it be a comforting Blackberry Cobbler to chase away autumn blues, a Watermelon Sorbet to celebrate a lazy summer's day or a Chocolate Pavlova with Chocolate Curls to bring your dinner party to a memorable finale.

When planning a menu, choose a dessert to complement the preceding courses. A hearty casserole calls for a simple sorbet or fruit salad, whereas a plainly grilled fish dish could precede something rich and creamy, for instance an Amaretto Soufflé or a Minted Raspberry Bavarois. If you plan to spoil your guests with a self-indulgent masterpiece such as Hazelnut Meringue Torte with Pears, then keep the rest of the meal as low key as possible.

When serving eight or more, it is a good idea to offer a choice of desserts. These should contrast in colour and content, so perhaps offer a fruity Autumn Pudding alongside a Chocolate Loaf with Coffee Sauce. Where appropriate, offer a choice of accompaniments, such as Greek-style yogurt and clotted cream. Fresh fruit is always a favourite and there are plenty of ideas here for both hot and cold desserts. One simple idea for serving fruit used in Thai cookery is to cut fresh pineapple, melon and papaya into similar-sized wedges and overlap them on a decorative platter with orange and pink grapefruit segments around the rim.

Ice cream desserts can be as simple or as elaborate as you like. Making your own ice cream also means that you control the ingredients as well as the cost. Yogurt, buttermilk or fromage frais will make lower-calorie versions, liqueurs can be added to please dinner party guests and fruit purées can be transformed into luscious sorbets. After a rich meal, serve a simple water ice or a granita. Parties call for sumptuous parfaits — ice cream or whipped cream layered in a tall glass with chocolate or fruit, and then frozen — or sundaes that are assembled at the last minute.

Decorating desserts can be a creative exercise. The most ordinary mousse surrounded by a fresh fruit coulis feathered with

cream looks exquisite, while rosettes of cream spiked with chocolate leaves would make the perfect topping for a rich mocha mousse. Another idea is to use the main ingredient in the dessert, decorating a strawberry cheesecake with chocolate-tipped strawberries for example, or Oranges in Caramel Sauce with strips of blanched orange peel.

This recipe collection ranges from fruity desserts to classic custards, and also includes classic favourites such as Fruity Bread Pudding, Baked Caramel Custard and Cherry Batter Pudding. Coffee and chocolate desserts get a chapter to themselves, and with Coffee Jellies with Amaretti Cream and Chocolate Cream Puffs on offer, you may be sure everyone will get more than their just desserts!

7

Ingredients

BUTTER

Use unsalted butter for desserts. Store it in the fridge, in the original wrapper. Freeze unopened packets in a polythene bag for up to six months.

CHOCOLATE

Most supermarkets stock a good range of plain, milk and white chocolate and chocolate products, including sprinkles, chips and buttons. For the best results in cooking, use chocolate with a cocoa solid content of at least 50 per cent. Chocolate with a high cocoa butter content melts easily. Unsweetened cocoa powder is used in baking.

COFFEE

Coffee adds a rich, unmistakable flavour to cakes, desserts and ice cream. It is used in instant powder or crushed granular form for cakes and biscuits. For a rich dessert, use a coffee liqueur such as Tia Maria for flavouring and decorate the dessert with coffee beans dipped in chocolate.

CREAM

Single cream has 18 per cent butterfat and is mainly used for pouring. In whipping cream the butterfat content increases to 35–38 per cent. When whipped, the cream will hold its shape briefly, but for a dessert decoration, use double cream (48 per cent butterfat). Crème fraîche is a thick, soured cream made from single cream, but with less fat.

EGGS

Unless recipes specify otherwise, use medium-size eggs. Always buy eggs from a reputable supplier, preferably date-stamped, and use them fresh. This is important when the eggs in a recipe are not cooked.

SUGAR

The darker the sugar, the stronger the flavour of molasses you will taste. Useful choices for desserts are golden caster sugar, demerara sugar, and light and dark muscovado sugars. Icing sugar is also useful for lightly sprinkling over finished desserts.

Fruits

CITRUS FRUITS

Lemons and limes are interchangeable in most recipes, but lime is more scented and has an intense flavour, so use it more sparingly. Oranges are available year-round and a good choice for desserts – use the rind or juice, or cut the fruit into segments. Satsumas, tangerines, mandarins and clementines are small citrus fruits which are interchangeable in most recipes.

STONE FRUITS

Use apricots raw or lightly poached. Cherries should be firm and glossy. Plums are available in dessert and cooking varieties. They range in colour from pale gold to black. For cooking, use slightly under-ripe plums. Choose white peaches for the sweetest flavour, and yellow for a more aromatic flavour.

SOFT FRUITS

Blackberries can be found growing wild or cultivated. Brambles are usually smaller than cultivated blackberries, with a stronger flavour. When they are not available, use raspberries or blackcurrants. Blackcurrants, redcurrants and white currants are usually sold "on the string", that is, on the stem. Keep a few on the stem for decoration. Raspberries, tayberries and loganberries are all delicious, juicy berries. Strawberries are best eaten fresh and ripe, they tend to lose texture and colour if frozen. Dessert gooseberries are sweet. Cooking varieties are smaller, firm, green and slightly sharp.

EXOTIC FRUITS

Figs are green-or purple-skinned fruit with sweet, pinkish-red flesh. Eat figs whole or peeled. Fresh dates are sweet and juicy, and are more succulent than dried dates. Kiwi fruit are available all year round. Peel them thinly and slice the bright-green flesh.

ORCHARD & VINE FRUITS

Apples and pears are versatile fruits; both dessert and culinary varieties can be cooked. Grapes are available in many varieties and vary in colour from pale green to deep purple. The sweetness varies, so taste before you buy.

Simple Sauces

APRICOT

Heat 225g/8oz/¾ cup apricot jam with 60ml/4 tbsp water. Allow to boil for 10 minutes, stirring continuously, then press through a sieve into a heatproof bowl. Stir in lemon juice to taste, and add a little orange-flavoured liqueur, if you like. Serve the sauce warm, poured over ice cream.

BUTTERSCOTCH

Melt 50g/2oz/4 tbsp butter with 115g/4oz/½ cup demerara sugar and 50g/2oz/3 tbsp golden syrup in a heavy-based saucepan over a medium heat. Bring the mixture to the boil, stirring constantly, then cook over a gentle heat until golden brown. Serve the sauce hot, over ice cream.

CHOCOLATE

Gently heat 150ml/¼ pint/⅔ cup double cream with 50g/2oz/4 tbsp diced butter and 50g/2oz/¼ cup caster sugar in a large saucepan, stirring until smooth. Allow to cool, then stir in 175g/6oz/1 cup chocolate chips or plain chocolate, broken into chunks, until melted and serve hot.

LEMON & LIME

Peel the rind from one lemon and two limes and squeeze the juice from the fruit. Place the rind in a saucepan, cover with water and bring to the boil. Drain through a sieve and reserve the rind. Mix 50g/2oz/¼ cup caster sugar in a bowl with 25ml/1½ tbsp arrowroot, and add a little water to give a smooth paste. Heat 175ml/6 fl oz/¾ cup of water, pour in the arrowroot, and stir until the sauce boils and thickens. Stir in 15ml/1 tbsp sugar, citrus juice and reserved rind, and serve hot. Sprinkle the dessert with fresh mint to decorate.

FRUIT COULIS

Wash and hull 450g/1lb/3 cups of raspberries, strawberries, or blackberries and drain them on kitchen paper. Purée the berries in a blender or food processor. Turn the machine on and off a few times and scrape down the bowl to be sure all the berries are evenly puréed. For soft berries with small seeds, press the purée through a fine-mesh nylon sieve. Add 25–50g/1–2oz/3–6 tbsp of sifted icing sugar to taste and a litttle lemon juice and/or 13–30ml/1–2 tbsp of liqueur. Stir well to dissolve the sugar completely.

Decorations

ALMONDS

Flaked and nibbed, plain or toasted, almonds look good on creamy desserts. To toast them, spread flaked almonds in a single layer in a grill pan and grill under a medium heat until golden brown. Shake the pan often and watch the nuts all the time as they burn very easily. Press them on to the sides of a cold soufflé.

CHOCOLATE CARAQUE

Pour melted chocolate on to a clean, smooth surface, such as a marble slab. When set, draw a broad-bladed cook's knife lightly across the chocolate at an angle of 45 degrees, to cut thin layers that curl into scrolls. Alternatively, use a potato peeler on a bar of chocolate.

PIPED CHOCOLATE

Pipe melted chocolate designs on non-stick baking paper. Spider webs, hearts and stars all look good, but lift them very carefully when transferring them to a cake or pudding.

CHOCOLATE LEAVES

Select clean, unblemished, non-poisonous leaves (rose leaves work well) and brush the undersides evenly with melted chocolate. Leave to set on non-stick baking paper, then carefully peel away the chocolate leaves from the green leaves.

ICING SUGAR/COCOA POWDER

Lay strips of paper or an old-fashioned paper doily over a dessert before dusting it with icing sugar and/or cocoa powder. Carefully remove the paper to give a striped effect.

WHIPPED CREAM

Swirls, shells and rosettes of whipped cream are easy to achieve. Use a piping bag fitted with a large, star-shaped nozzle and keep the pressure even. Try not to over-handle cream. Take care not to overwhip cream for piping as the cream will thicken further as it is forced out of the piping bag.

FROSTED FRUIT

For frosting fruit, have ready tiny bunches of grapes or blackcurrants, or stemmed cherries. Brush the fruits with water, then roll or dip them into caster sugar to coat. Allow to dry before using as a decoration. Unfrosted berry fruits also make perfect decorations.

CITRUS RIND

Top citrus sorbets with thinly pared orange, lemon or lime rind. Blanch the rind in boiling water, then drain and dry it thoroughly before use. Be sure to avoid the bitter white pith below the rind when preparing the fruit zest.

Techniques

WHISKING EGG WHITES

Separate the eggs carefully, by tapping the egg sharply against the edge of a mixing bowl. Hold the egg over the bowl and pull the two halves of the shell apart. Gently tip the yolk from one half to the other, allowing the white to run into the bowl. Place the egg whites in a clean, grease-free mixing bowl. Use a balloon whisk in a wide bowl for the greatest volume, although an electric hand whisk will also do an efficient job. Whisk the whites until they are firm enough to hold either soft or stiff peaks when you lift the whisk, according to the recipe's requirements. Use the mixture immediately.

MELTING CHOCOLATE

The best way to melt chocolate is over very hot but not boiling water. Break the chocolate into a heat-proof bowl. Bring a saucepan of water to the boil, turn off the heat and set the bowl on top. Stir as the chocolate melts. Do not add any liquid to melting chocolate, and do not cover it during or after melting because any water or condensation could cause the chocolate to seize or stiffen.

If you choose to melt chocolate in the microwave, check it at 5–10 second intervals, since it can burn easily. Place in a microwave-safe bowl and heat on medium power for 2 minutes.

WHIPPING CREAM

Cooks with strong wrists swear that a rotary whisk gives the greatest volume, but a hand-held electric mixer works well. Use double cream for decorations, and be careful not to overwhip the cream. It should just hold its shape and must not look grainy.

MAKING CHOCOLATE CASES

Chocolate cases make perfect containers for mousses. Use double cupcake cases or sweet cases. Using a brush or teaspoon, coat the inside of the inner case evenly with melted chocolate, invert, and leave to set. Peel away the paper and fill just before serving.

LINING A PASTRY TIN

A neat pastry case that doesn't distort or shrink in baking is the desired result. The key to success is handling the dough gently.

Remove the chilled dough from the fridge and allow it to soften slightly at room temperature. Place it on a lightly floured surface. Flatten the dough into a neat round. Lightly flour the rolling pin. Roll out the dough working from the centre to the edge and maintaining an even pressure. Lift and turn the dough from time to time to prevent it sticking to the surface. Continue until the dough is 5cm/2in larger all round than the tin and about 3mm/⅛in thick. Set the rolling pin on the dough near one side. Fold the outside edge of the dough over the pin, then roll the rolling pin over the dough to wrap the dough around it. Gently unroll the dough over the tin, centring it as much as possible. With your fingertips, lift and ease the dough into the tin, gently pressing it into place.

PEELING, CORING & SLICING APPLES

Cooking and eating apples are both very simple to prepare. Use a peeler to peel the fruit as thinly as possible, in a spiral movement, turning the fruit as you go.

Use a corer to press through the centre of the apple and pull it out to remove the core. Alternately, cut the apple in quarters and cut out the core from each quarter with a knife.

Cut the apple in quarters and slice across each segment to make slices an even thickness. Sprinkle with lemon juice to prevent them from browning.

13

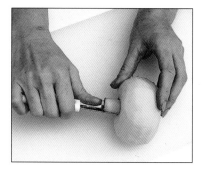

GRATING RIND FROM CITRUS FRUITS

The outer, coloured rind of citrus fruit, sometimes called the zest, is full of flavour, but the white pith is very bitter. Choose unwaxed fruits and wash and dry the fruit thoroughly before use. Use the fine gauge of a grater and rub the fruit against it to remove the coloured rind.

PREPARING SYRUP FOR A SORBET

Water ices and sorbets start with a simple syrup. Heat the sugar and water in a heavy-based saucepan over a medium heat, stirring gently until all the sugar is dissolved. Bring to the boil, and continue boiling without stirring for 2 minutes or for the time stated.

MAKING AN ICE BOWL

Ice creams and sorbets look spectacular in an ice bowl. Choose two freezerproof bowls, one about 7.5cm/3in wider than the other. Pour cold water into the larger bowl to two thirds full, and then centre the smaller bowl in the water, weighting it so that it floats level with the big bowl. Keep it in place with masking tape. Top up the surrounding water if necessary, and then freeze, adding flowers or leaves when the water is semi-frozen, if liked. Ease out the small bowl when frozen, release the ice bowl and store in the freezer until needed.

14

TIPS FOR PERFECT ICES

- *The faster you freeze ice cream, the fewer ice crystals will form, so turn the freezer to the coldest setting 1 hour before, or use the fast-freeze facility.*

- *Don't make too much at one time. Not only will this take too long, but it will also result in the formation of larger ice crystals.*

- *Constant churning in an ice-cream maker gives the creamiest results, but whisking by hand when ice crystals start to form, then once or twice more during freezing, is perfectly adequate.*

- *Home-made ice cream freezes hard. Allow it to soften before serving. This not only makes it easier to scoop but also gives the flavours a chance to "ripen".*

- *Add chunky flavourings such as chopped preserved ginger, nuts or chocolate chips, when the ice cream is partially frozen, or they will sink.*

- *Use a scoop or baller dipped in lukewarm water for shaping ice cream, or make simple ovals between two dessert spoons.*

PREPARING NUTS

To skin whole almonds, blanch them in boiling water for 2 minutes. Drain and cool slightly, then squeeze each to remove the skins. To skin hazelnuts and brazil nuts, toast in a 180°C/350°F/Gas 4 oven for 10–15 minutes, then rub the nuts in a tea towel to remove the skins.

To oven-toast or grill nuts, spread the nuts evenly on a baking sheet. Toast in a 180°C/350°F/Gas 4 oven or under the grill, until golden. Stir occasionally. To fry-toast nuts, put the nuts in a frying pan without fat. Toast over a moderate heat until golden brown, stirring constantly.

To grind nuts, use a nut mill or coffee grinder and grind a small batch at a time. Don't grind them too much as they will turn to a paste. You can also grind nuts in a food processor. To prevent turning the nuts to paste, grind then with some of the sugar or flour used in the recipe.

FLIPPING A PANCAKE

Pancakes are child's play if you use a good pan, grease it just sufficiently to prevent the batter from sticking, and pour in only enough batter to coat the base evenly. As the pancake sets, shake the pan to keep it from sticking. Check that it is lightly brown underneath, then hold the pan handle firmly, slide the pancake forward to the opposite rim and flip it over towards you with a neat flick of your wrist. Cook the pancake evenly on the second side, before sliding it out on to a plate and serving with your choice of filling.

15

PREPARING A SOUFFLE DISH

To make a cold soufflé that looks as though it has risen above the dish, use a smaller-than-necessary soufflé dish, adding a paper collar to hold the excess mixture in place. Cut a piece of non-stick baking paper slightly longer than the circumference of the dish and three times its depth. Fold it over length-ways, wrap it tightly around the outside of the dish and secure it firmly in place with string or freezer tape.

COOK'S TIP

It is not really necessary to make a paper collar for a hot soufflé. Instead, run a clean knife around the edge of the mixture, at a depth of 1cm/½in, to encourage even rising.

Cold Desserts

Chilled desserts are perfect to make when entertaining, since they can be prepared in advance. Plenty of classic dinner party dishes are included in this selection including Baked Caramel Custard and Minted Raspberry Bavarois, as well as innovative combinations and variations that are sure to impress. Try delicious Poached Pears in Maple-yogurt Sauce or for the figure-conscious Grapes in Grape-yogurt Jelly are a good choice. For everyday family meals try Autumn Pudding and substitute your choice of soft seasonal fruits.

Autumn Pudding

INGREDIENTS

10 slices white or brown bread, at least 1 day old
1 Bramley cooking apple, peeled, cored and sliced
225g/8oz ripe red plums, halved and stoned
225g/8oz/2 cups blackberries
60ml/4 tbsp water
75g/3oz/6 tbsp caster sugar
yogurt or fromage frais, to serve

SERVES 6

18

1 Slice off the crusts from the bread and use a biscuit cutter to stamp out a 7.5cm/3in round from one slice. Cut all the remaining slices in half.

2 Put the bread round in the base of a 1.2 litre/ 2 pint/5 cup pudding basin, then overlap the halves around the sides, saving some for the top.

3 Place the fruit, water and sugar in a pan, heat gently until the sugar dissolves, then simmer for 10 minutes, until soft. Drain, reserving the juice.

4 Spoon the fruit into the basin. Top with the reserved bread and spoon over the reserved juice.

5 Cover the basin with a saucer and place a weight on top of it. Chill the pudding overnight. Turn out on to a serving plate and serve with yogurt or fromage frais.

Poached Pears in Maple-yogurt Sauce

INGREDIENTS

6 firm dessert pears
15ml/1 tbsp lemon juice
250ml/8fl oz/1 cup sweet white wine or cider
thinly pared rind of 1 lemon
1 cinnamon stick
30ml/2 tbsp maple syrup
2.5ml/½ tsp arrowroot
150ml/¼ pint/⅔ cup Greek yogurt

SERVES 6

1 Thinly peel the pears, leaving them whole and with the stalks on. Brush with lemon juice, to prevent them from browning. Using a potato peeler or small knife, scoop out the core from the base of each pear and discard it.

2 Place the pears in a wide, heavy-based saucepan and pour over the wine, with enough cold water to almost cover the pears.

3 Add the pared lemon rind and cinnamon stick, then bring to the boil. Reduce the heat, cover the pan and simmer for about 30–40 minutes, or until all the pears are tender. Turn them occasionally so that they cook evenly. Lift out the pears carefully, with a large spoon, draining them well.

4 Bring the remaining liquid to the boil. Boil, uncovered, to reduce to about 120ml/4fl oz/ ½ cup. Strain, and add the maple syrup. Blend some of the liquid with the arrowroot. Return to the pan and cook, stirring, until thick and clear. Cool.

5 Slice each pear about three-quarters of the way through, leaving the slices attached at the stem end. Fan out each pear on a serving plate.

6 Stir 30ml/2 tbsp of the cooled syrup into the Greek yogurt and spoon it around each pear on the plates. Drizzle with the remaining syrup and serve the pears immediately.

19

Oranges in Caramel Sauce

3 Using a sharp vegetable knife, slice all the peeled fruit crossways into rounds about 1cm/½in thick. Put the orange slices in a serving bowl and pour over any juice.

4 Half-fill a large bowl with cold water and set aside. Place the sugar and 45ml/3 tbsp water in a small heavy-based pan without a non-stick coating. Bring it to the boil over a high heat, swirling the pan to dissolve all the sugar. Boil, without stirring, until the mixture turns a dark caramel colour. Remove the pan from the heat and, standing well back, dip the base of the pan into the bowl of cold water in order to stop the cooking process.

INGREDIENTS

6 large unwaxed seedless oranges
90g/3½oz/½ cup granulated sugar

SERVES 6

1 Using a vegetable peeler, remove wide strips of rind from two of the oranges. Stack two or three strips on top of each other and cut them into very thin julienne strips.

2 Cut a slice from the top and the base of each orange. Cut off the peel in strips from the top to the base, following the contours of the fruit.

5 Add 30ml/2 tbsp water to the caramel, pouring it down the sides of the pan, and swirling it to mix it thoroughly. Add the strips of orange rind and return the pan to the heat. Simmer over a medium-low heat for 8–10 minutes until the orange strips are slightly translucent, stirring occasionally.

6 Pour the caramel and rind over the orange slices in the serving bowl, turn gently to mix everything together and chill for at least 1 hour before serving.

20

Grapes in Grape-yogurt Jelly

INGREDIENTS

200g / 7oz / 1½ cups white seedless grapes
450ml / ¾ pint / scant 2 cups white grape juice
15ml / 1 tbsp / 1 sachet powdered gelatine
120ml / 4fl oz / ½ cup natural yogurt

SERVES 4

1 Reserve four sprigs of grapes for decoration and then cut the rest in half.

2 Divide the grapes between four stemmed glasses and tilt the glasses on one side, propping them firmly in a bowl of ice.

3 Place the grape juice in a pan and heat it until almost boiling. Remove from the heat and sprinkle the powdered gelatine over it, stirring until it all dissolves.

4 Pour half the grape juice over the grapes in the tilted glasses and allow to set.

5 Cool the remaining grape juice but do not allow to set, then stir it into the yogurt.

6 Stand the four set glasses upright and divide the yogurt mixture among them. Chill to set, then top each one with a sprig of grapes before serving.

Apples & Raspberries in Rose Pouchong Syrup

INGREDIENTS

5ml / 1 tsp rose pouchong tea
5ml / 1 tsp rose water (optional)
50g / 2oz / ¼ cup granulated sugar
5ml / 1 tsp lemon juice
5 dessert apples
175g / 6oz / 1 cup fresh raspberries

SERVES 4

1 Warm a large teapot. Add the tea and 900ml/ 1½ pints/3¾ cups of boiling water together with the rose water, if liked. Allow to infuse for 4 minutes.

2 Place the sugar and lemon juice in a large stainless steel saucepan. Carefully strain in all the infused rose pouchong tea and stir well until the sugar dissolves.

3 Peel, core and quarter the apples. Poach them in the syrup for about 5 minutes, then transfer the apples and syrup to a large metal tray and leave to cool.

4 Pour the cooled apples and rose pouchong syrup into a mixing bowl and add the fresh raspberries. Mix together well to combine all the ingredients, then spoon the fruit mixture into individual serving dishes or bowls and serve at room temperature.

COOK'S TIP

If fresh raspberries are out of season, use the same weight of frozen fruit or a 400g/14oz can of fruit, drained well.

Fresh Fruit with Mango Sauce

INGREDIENTS

1 large ripe mango, peeled, stoned and chopped
rind of 1 unwaxed orange
juice of 3 oranges
caster sugar, to taste
2 peaches
2 nectarines
1 small mango, peeled
2 plums
1 pear or ½ small melon
juice of 1 lemon
25-50g / 1-2oz / 2 heaped tbsp wild
strawberries (optional)
25-50g / 1-2oz / 2 heaped tbsp raspberries
25-50g / 1-2oz / 2 heaped tbsp blueberries
small mint sprigs, to decorate

SERVES 6

1 In a food processor fitted with a metal blade, process the large mango until smooth. Add the orange rind, juice and sugar to taste and process again until very smooth. Press through a sieve into a bowl. Chill the sauce until needed.

2 Peel the peaches, if liked, then stone and slice the peaches, nectarines, small mango and plums. Peel and quarter the pear, if using, and remove the core. Alternatively, deseed and slice the half melon thinly and remove all the peel.

3 Place all the sliced fruits on a large plate and sprinkle with the lemon juice to prevent any of them from discolouring. Chill the plate of fruit, covered with clear film, for up to 3 hours before completing the preparation for serving.

4 To serve the fruits, arrange the slices on individual serving plates and spoon the strawberries, if using, raspberries and blueberries over the top. Drizzle with a little of the fresh mango sauce and decorate the plates with mint sprigs. Serve the remaining mango sauce separately.

Cowslip Syllabub

INGREDIENTS

200ml / 7fl oz medium white wine
50g / 2oz / 4 tbsp caster (superfine) sugar
finely grated rind of 1 orange
juice of 1 orange
300ml / ½ pint double (heavy) cream
32 cowslip flowers, fresh or crystallized
8 viola flowers, fresh or crystallized
fresh mint sprigs, to decorate
langue de chat biscuits, to serve

SERVES 6

1 To make the syllabub, place the wine, sugar, orange rind and orange juice in a bowl. Leave the mixture to stand for at least 2 hours.

2 Add the mixture to the cream a little at a time, whisking constantly until it stands in soft peaks. Spoon a little of the syllabub into the base of six serving glasses, and sprinkle a few of the cowslips and violas around the edges.

3 Continue to spoon the syllabub into the glasses to form a peak in the centre. Scatter with more of the flowers and chill in the fridge. Fix any remaining flowers to the langue de chat biscuits with a dab of icing, and serve the syllabub with the decorated biscuits.

4 For the crystallized flowers, coat the petals with a thin, even layer of lightly beaten egg white. Use tweezers to dip the flowers into the egg white. The process must be done quickly before the egg white dries.

5 Sprinkle sifted icing (confectioners') sugar over the flowers, shaking off any excess. Uneven patches create an attractive light and dark shade contrast but the flowers will not be preserved as efficiently.

6 Allow the coated flowers to dry. Store carefully between layers of tissue paper in a cool, dry place, for up to a week. Do not refrigerate the petals.

Baked Caramel Custard

INGREDIENTS

250g / 9oz / scant 1¼ cups granulated sugar
60ml / 4 tbsp water
1 vanilla pod
400ml / 14fl oz / 1⅔ cups milk
250ml / 8fl oz / 1 cup whipping cream
5 large eggs
2 egg yolks

SERVES 6–8

1 Put 175g/6oz/¾ cup of the sugar in a small heavy saucepan with the water to moisten. Bring to the boil over a high heat, swirling the pan until the sugar dissolves. Boil, without stirring, until the syrup turns a dark caramel colour (this will take about 4–5 minutes).

2 Immediately pour the caramel into a 1 litre/ 1¾ pint/4 cup soufflé dish. Holding the dish with oven gloves, quickly swirl the dish to coat the base and sides with the caramel and set aside. (The caramel will harden quickly as it cools.) Place the dish in a small roasting tin. Preheat the oven to 160°C/325°F/Gas 3.

3 Split the vanilla pod lengthways and scrape the black seeds into a saucepan. Add the milk and cream. Bring to the boil over a medium-high heat, stirring  frequently. Remove the pan from the heat, cover and set aside for 15–20 minutes.

4 In a bowl, whisk the eggs and egg yolks with the remaining sugar for 2–3 minutes until smooth and creamy. Whisk in the hot milk. Strain the mixture into the caramel-lined dish. Cover with foil.

5 Pour enough boiling water into the roasting tin to come halfway up the sides of the dish. Bake the custard for 40–45 minutes until a knife inserted about 5cm/2in from the edge comes out clean (the custard should be just set). Remove from the roasting tin and cool for at least 30 minutes, then chill overnight.

6 To turn out, carefully run a sharp knife around the edge of the dish to loosen the custard. Cover the dish with an upturned plate. Holding them both tightly, invert the dish and plate together. Gently lift one edge of the dish, allowing the caramel to run over the sides, then slowly lift off the dish.

Minted Raspberry Bavarois

INGREDIENTS

*450g / 1lb / 3 cups fresh or frozen and
thawed raspberries*
30ml / 2 tbsp icing sugar
30ml / 2 tbsp lemon juice
15ml / 1 tbsp finely chopped fresh mint
30ml / 2 tbsp powdered gelatine
75ml / 5 tbsp boiling water
300ml / ½ pint / 1¼ cups custard
300ml / ½ pint / 1¼ cups Greek yogurt
fresh mint sprigs, to decorate

SERVES 6

3 Sprinkle 5ml/ 1 tsp of gelatine over 30ml/2 tbsp of boiling water and stir until it has dissolved. Add it to 150ml/¼ pint/ ⅔ cup of the raspberry fruit purée.

4 Pour this jelly into a 1 litre/1¾ pint/4 cup mould, and leave the mould to chill in the fridge until the jelly is just on the point of setting. Tip the mould to swirl the setting jelly around the sides, then leave to chill until the jelly has set completely.

1 Reserve some raspberries for decoration. Place the rest with the icing sugar and lemon juice in a food processor or blender. Process until smooth.

2 Pass the purée through a sieve to remove the raspberry seeds. Add the chopped fresh mint. You should have about 600ml/1 pint/2½ cups of purée.

5 Stir the rest of the fruit purée into the custard with the yogurt. Dissolve the rest of the gelatine in the rest of the water and stir it into the fruit.

6 Pour the custard into the mould and leave to chill until it has set. To serve, dip the mould quickly into hot water, then turn it out and decorate it with the reserved raspberries and the mint sprigs.

Baked Custard with Burnt Sugar

INGREDIENTS

1 vanilla pod
1 litre / 1¾ pints / 4 cups double cream
6 egg yolks
115g / 4oz / ½ cup caster sugar
30ml / 2 tbsp almond or orange liqueur
75g / 3oz / 6 tbsp soft light brown sugar

SERVES 6

1 Preheat the oven to 150°C/300°F/Gas 2. Place six 120ml/4fl oz/½ cup ramekins in a roasting tin or ovenproof dish and set aside.

2 Using a small sharp knife, split the vanilla pod lengthways and scrape the black seeds into a pan. Add the pod then add the cream and bring just to the boil over a medium-high heat, stirring frequently. Remove from the heat and cover. Set aside for about 15–20 minutes. Remove the vanilla pod.

3 In a bowl, whisk the egg yolks with the caster sugar and liqueur until well blended. Whisk in the hot cream and strain into a large jug. Divide among the ramekins.

4 Pour enough boiling water into the roasting tin to come halfway up the sides of the ramekin dishes. Cover the tin with foil and bake for about 30 minutes in the preheated oven until the custards are just set. Remove from the tin and leave to cool. Empty the water from the roasting tin, place the ramekins in it again and set aside to chill.

5 Preheat the grill. Sprinkle the soft light brown sugar evenly over the surface of each custard and grill for 30–60 seconds until the sugar melts and caramelizes. (Do not let the sugar burn or the custard curdle.) Place the baked custards in the fridge to set the crust thoroughly and chill the custard completely before serving.

Hot Desserts

On chilly days few things are more appealing than a warming pudding and there are recipes here for every occasion. Family favourites include Blackberry Cobbler, Gingerbread Upside Down Pudding, and Pear & Blueberry Pie. If you are looking for a new and enticing idea, try quick and tasty Apple Soufflé Omelette or Cherry Pancakes. For special occasions or for sheer indulgence, the elegant Amaretto Soufflé is easier than you might imagine, and Plum Filo Pockets, although a little fiddly, always look sensational.

Cherry Batter Pudding

INGREDIENTS

450g / 1lb ripe cherries
30ml / 2 tbsp kirsch or fruit brandy or
15ml / 1 tbsp lemon juice
15ml / 1 tbsp icing sugar
45ml / 3 tbsp plain flour
45ml / 3 tbsp granulated sugar
175ml / 6fl oz / ¾ cup milk or single cream
2 eggs
grated rind of ½ lemon
pinch of freshly grated nutmeg
1.5ml / ¼ tsp vanilla essence

SERVES 4

1 Stone the ripe cherries, if you like. Combine them in a mixing bowl with the kirsch, fruit brandy or lemon juice and icing sugar. Set aside for about 1–2 hours.

2 Preheat the oven to 190°C/375°F/Gas 5. Generously butter a 28cm/11in oval gratin dish or other shallow ovenproof dish.

3 Sift the flour into a bowl. Add the sugar. Slowly whisk in the milk or cream until smoothly blended. Add the eggs, lemon rind, nutmeg and vanilla essence and whisk until well combined and smooth.

4 Scatter the cherries evenly in the baking dish. Pour over the batter and bake in the preheated oven for 45 minutes, or until the pudding is set and puffed

around the edges; it is ready when a knife inserted in the centre comes out clean. Serve either warm or at room temperature.

Chocolate, Date & Walnut Pudding

1 First, grease a 1.2 litre/2 pint/ 5 cup pudding basin and place a small circle of non-stick baking or greaseproof paper in the base. Spoon in all the chopped walnuts and dates. Preheat the oven to 180°C/350°F/Gas 4.

2 Separate the eggs and place the yolks in a mixing bowl, with the vanilla essence and sugar. Place the bowl over a pan of hot water and whisk until the mixture is thick and pale.

3 Sift the flour and cocoa into the mixture and fold them in with a metal spoon. Stir in the milk, to soften the mixture slightly. Whisk the egg whites until they hold soft peaks and fold them in.

4 Spoon the mixture into the basin and bake for 40–45 minutes, or until risen and firm to the touch. Loosen the edge and turn the pudding out. Serve.

INGREDIENTS

25g/1oz/2 tbsp chopped walnuts
25g/1oz/2 tbsp chopped dates
2 eggs
5ml/1 tsp vanilla essence
30ml/2 tbsp golden caster sugar
45ml/3 tbsp wholemeal flour
15ml/1 tbsp cocoa powder
30ml/2 tbsp milk

SERVES 4

37

Creole Bread & Butter Pudding

INGREDIENTS

4 ready-to-eat dried apricots, chopped
15ml/1 tbsp raisins
30ml/2 tbsp sultanas
15ml/1 tbsp chopped mixed peel
1 French loaf (about 200g/7oz), thinly sliced
50g/2oz/4 tbsp butter, melted
115g/4oz/½ cup caster sugar
3 eggs
2.5ml/½ tsp vanilla essence
475ml/16fl oz/2 cups milk
150ml/¼ pint/⅔ cup double cream
30ml/2 tbsp rum
SAUCE
150ml/¼ pint/⅔ cup double cream
30ml/2 tbsp Greek yogurt
15-30ml/1-2 tbsp rum
15ml/1 tbsp caster sugar

SERVES 4–6

2 Whisk together the sugar, eggs and vanilla essence. Heat the milk and cream until just boiling and whisk into the eggs. Strain over the bread and fruit. Sprinkle the rum on top. Press the bread down, cover with foil and leave for 20 minutes.

1 Preheat the oven to 180°C/350°F/Gas 4. Lightly butter a deep 1.5 litre/2½ pint/6 cup oven-proof dish. Mix the dried fruits with the mixed peel and sprinkle a little over the base of the dish. Brush both sides of the bread slices with melted butter. Fill the dish with alternate layers of bread and dried fruit, finishing with a layer of bread.

3 Bake in a roasting tin half filled with boiling water for 1 hour or until the custard is set. Remove the foil and cook for 10 minutes more, until golden.

4 Warm all the sauce ingredients together in a small pan, stirring gently. Serve with the hot pudding.

Plum Pie

INGREDIENTS

275g / 10oz / 2½ cups plain flour
5ml / 1 tsp salt
75g / 3oz / ⅓ cup chilled unsalted butter
50g / 2oz / ½ cup chilled vegetable fat or lard
60-120ml / 4-8 tbsp iced water
milk, for glazing
FILLING
900g / 2lb red or purple plums,
halved and stoned
grated rind of 1 lemon
15ml / 1 tbsp lemon juice
115-175g / 4-6oz / ½-¾ cup caster sugar
45ml / 3 tbsp quick-cooking tapioca
pinch of salt
2.5ml / ½ tsp ground cinnamon
1.5ml / ¼ tsp grated nutmeg

SERVES 8

1 Sift the flour and salt into a bowl. Rub in the butter and vegetable fat or lard until the mixture resembles breadcrumbs. Stir in just enough iced water to bind the pastry. Gather into two balls, one slightly larger than the other. Wrap and chill for 20 minutes.

2 Preheat the oven to 220°C/425°F/Gas 7. Line a baking sheet with greaseproof paper. Set it aside. Roll out the larger piece of pastry to a thickness of about 3mm/⅛in and line a 23cm/9in pie dish.

3 Roll out the smaller piece of pastry to a round slightly larger than the top of the pie. Support it on the prepared baking sheet, then stamp out four hearts from the centre of the pastry, using a cutter. Reserve the pastry hearts.

4 Make the filling by mixing all the ingredients in a bowl. Use the larger quantity of sugar if the plums are very tart. Spoon the filling into the pastry case, then lift the pastry on the greaseproof paper and slide it into position over the filling. Trim and pinch to seal. Arrange the cut-out pastry hearts on top. Glaze the top of the pie with milk and bake for 15 minutes. Lower the oven temperature to 180°C/350°F/Gas 4 and bake for 30–35 minutes more, protecting the top with foil if needed.

Blackberry Cobbler

INGREDIENTS

675g/1½lb/6 cups blackberries
225g/8oz/1 cup caster sugar
45ml/3 tbsp plain flour
grated rind of 1 lemon
30ml/2 tbsp sugar mixed with 1.5ml/¼ tsp
grated nutmeg
TOPPING
225g/8oz/2 cups plain flour
225g/8oz/1 cup caster sugar
15ml/1 tbsp baking powder
1.5ml/¼ tsp salt
250ml/8fl oz/1 cup milk
115g/4oz/½ cup butter, melted

SERVES 8

1 First preheat the oven to 180°C/350°F/Gas 4. In a mixing bowl, combine all the blackberries with the caster sugar, flour and lemon rind. Stir gently to blend together before transferring to a 2.5 litre/4 pint/10 cup ovenproof dish.

2 To make the topping, sift the flour, sugar, baking powder, and salt into a large bowl. Set aside. Combine the milk and butter in a measuring jug.

3 Gradually stir the butter and milk mixture into the dry ingredients in the bowl and stir with a wooden spoon until the batter becomes smooth.

4 Spoon the batter over the fruit mix, spreading it right to the edges. Sprinkle the sugar and nutmeg mixture over the top, then bake in the preheated oven for about 50 minutes, until the batter topping is set and lightly browned. Serve hot.

Apple Soufflé Omelette

1 For the filling, gently sauté the apple slices in the butter and sugar until just tender. Stir in the single cream and keep warm, while you make the omelette.

2 Place the egg yolks in a bowl with the cream and sugar and beat well. Whisk the egg whites until stiff, then fold into the yolk mixture.

3 Melt the butter in a large heavy-based frying pan, pour in the soufflé mixture and spread it evenly. Cook for 1 minute until golden underneath, then place under a hot grill and brown the top.

4 Slide the omelette on to a plate, add the apple filling, then fold over. Sift the icing sugar over thickly, then press on a criss-cross pattern with a hot metal skewer. Serve immediately.

INGREDIENTS

4 eggs, separated
30ml/2 tbsp single cream
15ml/1 tbsp caster sugar
15g/½oz/1 tbsp butter
icing sugar, to decorate
FILLING
1 eating apple, peeled, cored and sliced
25g/1oz/2 tbsp butter
30ml/2 tbsp soft light brown sugar
45ml/3 tbsp single cream

SERVES 2

COOK'S TIP
For a summer variation, use fresh raspberries or strawberries instead of apples.

42

Plum Filo Pockets

INGREDIENTS

115g/4oz/½ cup soft cheese
15ml/1 tbsp light muscovado sugar
2.5ml/½ tsp ground cloves
8 large firm plums, halved and stoned
8 sheets filo pastry
sunflower oil, for brushing
icing sugar, to decorate

SERVES 4

1 First, preheat the oven to 220°C/ 425°F/Gas 7 and then mix together the soft cheese, muscovado sugar and cloves in a bowl. Stir well until combined.

2 Sandwich the plum halves back together with a spoonful of the cheese mixture. Spread out the pastry and cut into 16 pieces, about 23cm/9in square. Brush one lightly with oil and place a second on top diagonally. Repeat with the other squares.

3 Put a plum on each pastry square, and pinch the corners together. Put on a baking sheet and bake for 15–18 minutes, until golden. Dust with icing sugar.

43

Fruity Bread Pudding

44

2 Quickly remove the pan from the heat and carefully stir in all the diced bread, mixed spice and sliced banana. Mix well. Spoon this mixture into a shallow 1.2 litre/

2 pint/5 cup ovenproof baking dish and then pour the milk over the top in an even layer.

3 Sprinkle the top with the demerara sugar and bake in the hot oven for 25–30 minutes, until it is firm and golden brown. Serve hot or cold, with yogurt.

INGREDIENTS

75g/3oz/½ cup mixed dried fruit
150ml/¼ pint/⅔ cup apple juice
115g/4oz stale brown or white bread, diced
5ml/1 tsp mixed spice
1 large banana, sliced
150ml/¼ pint/⅔ cup milk
15ml/1 tbsp demerara sugar
natural yogurt, to serve

SERVES 4

1 Preheat the oven to 200°C/400°F/Gas 6. Place the dried fruit in a saucepan with the apple juice and bring to the boil.

COOK'S TIP
Different types of bread and its degree of staleness will cause variation in the amount of liquid absorbed, so you may need to adjust the amount of milk to allow for this.

Gingerbread Upside Down Pudding

INGREDIENTS

15ml/1 tbsp soft brown sugar
4 peaches, halved and stoned or 8 canned
peach halves
8 walnut halves
yogurt or custard, to serve
BASE
115g/4oz/1 cup wholemeal flour
7.5ml/1½ tsp ground ginger
2.5ml/½ tsp bicarbonate of soda
5ml/1 tsp ground cinnamon
115g/4oz/½ cup demerara sugar
1 egg
120ml/4fl oz/½ cup milk
50ml/2fl oz/¼ cup sunflower oil

SERVES 4–6

2 Arrange the peach halves cut-side down in the tin with a walnut half in each.

3 Make the base. Sift together the flour, ginger, bicarbonate of soda, and cinnamon, then stir in the sugar. Beat together the egg, milk and oil, then mix into the dry ingredients until smooth.

4 Pour the mixture evenly over the peaches and bake for 35–40 minutes, until firm to the touch. Turn out on to a serving plate. Serve hot with yogurt or custard.

45

1 First, preheat the oven to 180°C/350°F/Gas 4 and brush the base and sides of a 23cm/9in round spring-form tin with oil. Sprinkle the sugar over the base.

Cherry Lattice Pie

INGREDIENTS

*2 x 450g/1lb cans cherries, drained or
900g/2lb/4 cups pitted fresh cherries
75g/3oz/6 tbsp caster sugar
25g/1oz/1/4 cup plain flour
25ml/1 1/2 tbsp fresh lemon juice
1.5ml/1/4 tsp almond essence
25g/1oz/2 tbsp butter or margarine*
PASTRY
*225g/8oz/2 cups plain flour
5ml/1 tsp salt
175g/6oz/3/4 cup butter or margarine, diced
60-75ml/4-5 tbsp iced water*

SERVES 8

1 Make the pastry. Sift the flour and salt into a mixing bowl. Rub in the butter or margarine until the mixture resembles coarse breadcrumbs. Sprinkle in the iced water, 15ml/1 tbsp at a time, tossing with your fingertips until the dough forms a ball.

2 Divide the dough in half and shape each half into a ball. On a lightly floured surface, roll out one of the balls to a circle about 30cm/12in in diameter.

3 Use the dough circle to line a 23cm/9in pie dish, easing the dough in and being careful not to stretch it. Trim off all the excess dough, leaving a 1cm/1/2in overhang around the rim. Roll out the remaining dough to 3mm/1/8in thickness. With a sharp knife, cut out 11 strips, 1cm/1/2in wide.

4 In a mixing bowl, combine the cherries, sugar, flour, lemon juice and almond essence. Spoon the mixture into the pastry shell and dot the butter or margarine over the surface.

5 For the lattice, space five of the pastry strips over the cherry filling and fold every other strip back. Lay a strip across, perpendicular to the others. Fold  the strips back over the filling. Continue in this way, folding back every other strip each time you add a cross strip. Trim the ends of the lattice strips to make them even with the pastry overhang. Press together so that the edge rests on the pie dish rim. Flute the edge. Chill for 15 minutes. Preheat the oven to 220°C/425°F/Gas 7.

6 Bake the pie for 30 minutes, covering the edge with foil, if necessary, to prevent burning.

Cherry Pancakes

INGREDIENTS

PANCAKES
50g/2oz/½ cup plain flour
50g/2oz/½ cup plain wholemeal flour
pinch of salt
1 egg white
150ml/¼ pint/⅔ cup milk
150ml/¼ pint/⅔ cup water
a little oil for frying
fromage frais, to serve
FILLING
425g/15oz can black cherries in juice
7.5ml/1½ tsp arrowroot

SERVES 4

1 Sift the flours and salt into a bowl, adding any bran left in the sieve to the bowl.

2 Make a well in the centre of the flour and add the egg white. Gradually beat in the milk and water, whisking hard until all the flour and liquid is incorporated and the batter is smooth and bubbly.

3 Heat a non-stick pan with a small amount of oil until it is very hot. Pour in just enough batter to cover the base of the pan and swirl to cover it evenly.

4 Cook until the pancake is set and golden, and then turn to cook the other side. Remove to a sheet of kitchen paper and cook the remaining batter, to make about eight pancakes in all.

5 Drain the cherries, reserving the juice. Blend about 30ml/2 tbsp of the juice from the can of cherries with the arrowroot in a saucepan. Stir in the rest of the juice. Heat gently, stirring, until boiling. Stir the mixture over a moderate heat for about 2 minutes, until thickened and clear.

6 Add the cherries to the pan and stir until heated through. Spoon the cherry mixture into the pancakes, fold them in quarters and serve with fromage frais.

Amaretto Soufflé

INGREDIENTS

6 amaretti biscuits, coarsely crushed
90ml/6 tbsp Amaretto liqueur
4 eggs, separated, plus 1 egg white
*115g/4oz/½ cup caster sugar, plus extra
for sprinkling*
30ml/2 tbsp plain flour
250ml/8fl oz/1 cup milk
pinch of cream of tartar (optional)
icing sugar, for decorating

SERVES 6

1 Preheat the oven to 200°C/400°F/Gas 6. Butter a 1.5 litre/2½ pint/6 cup soufflé dish; sprinkle with caster sugar. Sprinkle the biscuits with 30ml/2 tbsp of the Amaretto liqueur and set aside.

2 Mix the 4 egg yolks with 30ml/ 2 tbsp of the caster sugar and the flour. Stir until smooth. Put the milk in a heavy saucepan and heat it just to the boil. Remove from the heat and gradually add the hot milk to the beaten egg mixture, stirring.

3 Pour the milk and egg mixture back into the pan. Set it over a medium-low heat and simmer gently for 4 minutes or until thickened, stirring constantly. Add the remaining Amaretto liqueur and remove the pan from the heat.

4 In a scrupulously clean, grease-free bowl, whisk the 5 egg whites until they form soft peaks. (If not using a copper bowl, add the cream of tartar as soon as the whites are frothy.) Add the remaining sugar and continue whisking until stiff.

5 Add about one-quarter of the whites to the liqueur mixture and stir in with a rubber spatula. Add the remaining whites and fold in gently.

6 Spoon half the mixture into the prepared dish. Cover with a layer of the moistened amaretti biscuits, then spoon the remaining soufflé mixture evenly on the top.

7 Bake the dish for 20 minutes in the preheated oven or until the soufflé is risen and lightly browned on top. Sprinkle with sifted icing sugar and serve immediately.

Pear & Blueberry Pie

Ingredients

675g/1½lb/6 cups blueberries
30ml/2 tbsp caster sugar
15ml/1 tbsp arrowroot
2 ripe but firm pears, peeled, cored and sliced
2.5ml/½ tsp ground cinnamon
grated rind of ½ lemon
beaten egg, to glaze
caster sugar, for sprinkling
crème fraîche, to serve
Pastry
225g/8oz/2 cups plain flour
pinch of salt
50g/2oz/4 tbsp lard, cubed
50g/2oz/4 tbsp butter, cubed

Serves 4

1 Make the pastry. Sift the flour and salt into a bowl and rub in the fats. Stir in 45ml/3 tbsp cold water and mix to a dough. Chill for 30 minutes.

2 Place 225g/8oz/2 cups of the blueberries in a pan with the sugar. Cover and cook gently until the blueberries have softened. Press through a sieve.

3 Blend the arrowroot with 30ml/2 tbsp cold water and add to the blueberry purée. Place in a small saucepan and bring to the boil, stirring until thickened. Cool the mixture slightly.

4 Place a baking sheet in the oven and preheat to 190°C/375°F/ Gas 5. Roll out just over half the pastry on a lightly floured surface and use to line a 20cm/8in shallow pie dish or plate; do this by lopping the pastry over the rolling pin and lifting into position.

5 Mix together the remaining blueberries, the pears, cinnamon and lemon rind and spoon into the dish. Pour the blueberry purée over the top.

6 Roll out the remaining pastry to just larger than the pie dish and lay over the filling. Press the edges together to seal, then trim off any excess pastry and crimp the edge. Make a small slit in the centre to allow steam to escape. Brush with egg and sprinkle with caster sugar. Bake the pie on the hot baking sheet for 40–45 minutes, until golden. Serve warm with crème fraîche.

Baked Blackberry Cheesecake

INGREDIENTS

175g/6oz/¾ cup cottage cheese
150g/5oz/⅔ cup low-fat natural yogurt
15ml/1 tbsp plain wholemeal flour
25g/1oz/2 tbsp golden caster sugar
1 egg
1 egg white
finely grated rind and juice of ½ lemon
200g/7oz/2 cups fresh or frozen and thawed blackberries

SERVES 5

54

4 Tip the mixture into the prepared tin and bake it for 30–35 minutes or until it's just set. Turn off the oven and leave for a further 30 minutes.

1 First, preheat the oven to 180°C/350°F/ Gas 4. Then lightly grease and base-line an 18 cm/7 in sandwich tin.

2 Place the cottage cheese in a food processor and process until smooth. Alternatively, rub it through a sieve, to obtain a smooth mixture.

3 Add the yogurt, flour, sugar, egg and egg white and mix. Add the lemon rind, juice and blackberries, reserving a few for decoration.

5 Run a knife around the edge of the cheesecake and then turn it out. Remove the lining paper and place the cheesecake on a warm serving plate.

6 Decorate the cheesecake with the reserved blackberries and serve it warm.

Chocolate & Coffee

Rich, creamy chocolate desserts are a sure winner whatever the occasion. This indulgent ingredient is guaranteed to turn any dish into a wicked temptation. Try Chocolate Cheesecake Pie decorated with swirls of whipped cream and curls of solid plain or milk chocolate, or team this heavenly ingredient with the unmistakable flavour of coffee. Chocolate Loaf with Coffee Sauce successfully combines the two flavours and makes a feast for a special occasion. For a rich and smooth dessert try Luxury Mocha Mousse served with chocolate coffee beans.

French Chocolate Cake

INGREDIENTS

225g/8oz/1 cup unsalted butter,
cut into pieces
250g/9oz plain chocolate, chopped
115g/4oz/½ cup granulated sugar
30ml/2 tbsp brandy or orange-flavour liqueur
5 eggs
15ml/1 tbsp plain flour
icing sugar, to decorate
sour cream and cherries, to serve

SERVES 10

1 Preheat the oven to 180°C/350°F/Gas 4. Base-line and grease a 23 x 5cm/9 x 2in springform tin. Wrap foil around the tin so it is water-tight.

2 Stir the butter, the chocolate and sugar over a low heat until smooth. Cool slightly. Stir in the liqueur. In a mixing bowl, beat the eggs lightly, then beat in the flour. Slowly beat in the chocolate mixture until blended. Pour into the tin, smoothing the surface.

3 Place the springform tin in a roasting tin and pour in boiling water to come 2cm/¾in up the side of the springform tin. Bake for 25–30 minutes until the edge of the cake is set, but the centre is still soft. Remove the foil. Cool in the tin on a wire rack (the cake will sink and may crack).

4 Turn the cake on to a wire rack. Remove the springform tin bottom and paper, so the bottom of the cake is now the top.

5 Cut 6–8 strips of non-stick baking paper 2.5cm/1in wide and place them randomly over the cake, or make a lattice-style pattern if you wish. Dust the cake with icing sugar, then carefully remove the paper. Slide the cake on to a serving plate and serve with sour cream and fresh cherries.

Coffee Jellies with Amaretti Cream

INGREDIENTS

75g / 3oz / 6 tbsp caster sugar
450ml / ¾ pint / scant 2 cups hot strong coffee
30-45ml / 2-3 tbsp dark rum or coffee liqueur
20ml / 4 tsp powdered gelatine
COFFEE AMARETTI CREAM
150ml / ¼ pint / ⅔ cup double or
whipping cream
15ml / 1 tbsp icing sugar, sifted
10-15ml / 2-3 tsp instant coffee granules
dissolved in 15ml / 1 tbsp hot water
6 large amaretti biscuits, crushed

SERVES 4

1 Put the sugar in a saucepan with 75ml/5 tbsp water and stir over a gentle heat until dissolved. Increase the heat; allow the syrup to boil steadily, without stirring, for 3–4 minutes.

2 Stir all the hot coffee and rum or coffee liqueur into the hot syrup. Sprinkle the powdered gelatine over the top and stir until it dissolves completely.

3 Pour the coffee jelly mixture into four wetted 150ml/¼ pint/⅔ cup moulds and allow them to cool thoroughly, before placing them in the fridge. Leave the jellies in the fridge for several hours until they are completely set.

4 To make the amaretti cream, lightly whip the cream with the icing sugar until it holds stiff peaks. Stir in the instant coffee, then gently fold in all but 30ml/2 tbsp of the crushed amaretti biscuits.

5 Remove the jellies from their moulds and place on four individual serving plates. Spoon a little of the coffee amaretti cream to one side of each jelly. Dust over the reserved amaretti biscuit crumbs and serve the dessert at once.

Luxury White Chocolate Cheesecake

INGREDIENTS

150g/5oz (about 16-18) digestive biscuits
50g/2oz/½ cup blanched hazelnuts, toasted
50g/2oz/4 tbsp unsalted butter, melted
2.5ml/½ tsp ground cinnamon
FILLING
350g/12oz fine quality white chocolate, chopped
120ml/4fl oz/½ cup whipping or
double cream
675g/1½lb/3 x 8oz packets cream
cheese, softened
50g/2oz/¼ cup granulated sugar
4 eggs
15ml/1 tbsp vanilla essence
TOPPING
450ml/¾ pint/scant 2 cups soured cream
50g/2oz/¼ cup granulated sugar
15ml/1 tbsp hazelnut-flavour liqueur or
5ml/1 tsp vanilla essence
white chocolate curls, to decorate
cocoa, for dusting (optional)

SERVES 16–20

1 Preheat the oven to 180°C/350°F/Gas 4 and grease a 23 x 7.5cm/9 x 3in springform tin. Process the biscuits and hazelnuts to fine crumbs, then mix with the butter and cinnamon. Press the mixture on to the bottom and sides of the tin and bake for 5–7 minutes, or until just set.

2 Lower the oven to 150°C/300°F/Gas 2. Make the filling. Melt the chocolate and cream over a low heat until smooth, stirring frequently. Cool.

3 Beat the cream cheese and sugar until smooth; beat in the eggs, one at a time, the white chocolate mixture and vanilla. Pour into the baked crust and bake for  45–55 minutes, or until the edge of the filling is firm but the centre is still slightly soft. Transfer to a wire rack, still in its tin, and increase the oven to 200°C/400°F/Gas 6.

4 Make the topping. Whisk the soured cream with the sugar and liqueur or vanilla and pour it over the cheesecake, spreading it evenly. Return the cheesecake to the oven for 5–7 minutes. Turn off the oven, but do not open the door for 1 hour.

5 Transfer the cheesecake to a wire rack to cool in the tin. Remove the tin, then chill the cheesecake, loosely covered, overnight.

6 Place the cheesecake on a serving plate. Decorate the top with chocolate curls and dust lightly with cocoa, if liked.

60

Chocolate Pavlova with Chocolate Curls

INGREDIENTS

275g/10oz/2½ cups icing sugar
15ml/1 tbsp unsweetened cocoa
5ml/1 tsp cornflour
5 egg whites, at room temperature
pinch of salt
5ml/1 tsp cider vinegar or lemon juice
CHOCOLATE CREAM
175g/6oz plain chocolate, chopped
120ml/4fl oz/½ cup milk
25g/1oz/2 tbsp butter, diced
30ml/2 tbsp brandy
475ml/16fl oz/2 cups double cream
TOPPING
450g/1lb/4 cups mixed berries or diced
mango, papaya, lychees and pineapple
chocolate curls
icing sugar

SERVES 8–10

1 Preheat the oven to 160°C/325°F/Gas 3. Place a sheet of non-stick baking paper on to a baking sheet and mark a 20cm/8in circle on it. Sift 45ml/3 tbsp of the icing sugar with the cocoa and cornflour and set aside. Using an electric mixer, beat the egg whites until frothy. Add the salt and beat until the whites form stiff peaks.

2 Sprinkle the remaining icing sugar into the egg whites, a little at a time, making sure each addition is dissolved before beating in the next. Fold in the cornflour mixture, then quickly fold in the vinegar or lemon juice.

3 Now spoon the mixture on to the paper circle, with the sides higher than the centre. Bake for 1 hour, until set, then turn off the oven but leave the meringue inside for 1 hour longer. Remove from the oven, peel off the paper and leave to cool.

4 Make the chocolate cream. Melt the chocolate and milk over a low heat, stirring until smooth. Remove from the heat and whisk in the butter and brandy. Cool for 1 hour.

5 Transfer the meringue to a serving plate. When the chocolate mixture has cooled, but is not too firm, beat the cream until soft peaks form. Stir half the cream into the chocolate mixture to lighten it, then fold in the remaining cream. Spoon it into the centre of the meringue. Arrange fruit and chocolate curls in the centre of the meringue, over the cream. Dust with icing sugar.

Chocolate Cream Puffs

INGREDIENTS

250ml / 8fl oz / 1 cup water
2.5ml / ½ tsp salt
15ml / 1 tbsp granulated sugar
115g / 4oz / ½ cup unsalted butter, diced
150g / 5oz / 1¼ cups plain flour, sifted
30ml / 2 tbsp unsweetened cocoa, sifted
4–5 eggs
*1 quantity Chocolate Cream (page 62),
for filling*
GLAZE
300ml / ½ pint / 1¼ cups whipping cream
50g / 2oz / 4 tbsp unsalted butter, diced
15ml / 1 tbsp corn or golden syrup
225g / 8oz plain chocolate, chopped
5ml / 1 tsp vanilla essence

MAKES 12

1 Preheat the oven to 220°C/425°F/Gas 7. Grease a baking sheet. Bring the water, salt, sugar and butter to the boil. Remove from the heat; tip in the flour and cocoa. Stir vigorously until the mixture leaves the sides of the pan. Cook for 1 minute, beating constantly. Remove from the heat.

2 Beat in four of the eggs, one at a time. The mixture should be thick, smooth and shiny and fall from a spoon. If it is too dry, beat the fifth egg and beat it into the mixture gradually. Spoon the batter into an icing bag with a star tip and pipe 12 puffs on the prepared baking sheet.

3 Bake the puffs for 35–40 minutes until puffed and firm. Slice off the top third of each puff and return both tops and bottoms, cut-side up, to the baking sheet. Cook for a few minutes more, to dry out. Cool on a wire rack.

4 Spoon the chocolate cream into a piping bag fitted with a plain tip. Fill the bottom of each puff, then cover with a top.

5 Make the glaze. Melt the cream, butter, syrup, chocolate and vanilla until smooth, stirring often. Remove from the heat and leave to cool for about 20–30 minutes, until slightly thickened. Pour a little glaze over each of the cream puffs, or dip the top of each puff into the glaze, and leave to set. To serve, arrange the puffs on a serving plate in a single layer or pile them up on top of each other.

Chocolate Loaf with Coffee Sauce

INGREDIENTS

175g/6oz plain chocolate, chopped
50g/2oz/4 tbsp butter, softened
4 large eggs, separated
30ml/2 tbsp rum or brandy (optional)
pinch of cream of tartar
chocolate curls and chocolate coffee beans,
to decorate
COFFEE SAUCE
600ml/1 pint/2½ cups milk
9 egg yolks
50g/2oz/¼ cup caster sugar
5ml/1 tsp vanilla essence
15ml/1 tbsp instant coffee powder, dissolved
in 30ml/2 tbsp hot water

SERVES 6–8

1 Line a 1.2 litre/2 pint/5 cup loaf tin with clear film. Place the plain chocolate in a bowl set over hot water and leave for 3–5 minutes, then stir.

2 Remove the bowl from the pan and quickly beat in the butter, egg yolks, one at a time, and rum or brandy, if using.

3 In a clean grease-free bowl, using an electric mixer, beat the egg whites slowly until frothy. Add the cream of tartar, increase the speed and continue beating until they form soft peaks, then stiffer peaks that just flop over a little. Stir one-third of the egg whites into the chocolate mixture, then fold in the remaining whites. Pour into the lined loaf tin and smooth the top. Cover and freeze until ready to serve.

4 Make the coffee sauce. Bring the milk to a simmer over a medium heat. Whisk the egg yolks and the sugar for 2–3 minutes until thick and creamy, then whisk in the hot milk and return the mixture to the saucepan. With a wooden spoon, stir over a low heat until the sauce begins to thicken and coat the back of the spoon. Strain the custard into a chilled bowl, stir in the vanilla essence and coffee and set aside to cool, stirring occasionally. Chill.

5 To serve, uncover the loaf tin and dip the base into hot water for 10 seconds. Invert the chocolate loaf on to a board and peel off the clear film. Cut the loaf into slices and serve with the coffee sauce. Decorate with the chocolate curls and chocolate coffee beans.

Hazelnut Meringue Torte with Pears

INGREDIENTS

175g/6oz/¾ cup granulated sugar
1 vanilla pod, split
475ml/16fl oz/2 cups water
4 ripe pears, peeled, halved and cored
6 egg whites
275g/10oz/2½ cups icing sugar
175g/6oz/1¼ cups ground hazelnuts
5ml/1 tsp vanilla essence
50g/2oz plain chocolate, melted
chocolate caraque, to decorate
CHOCOLATE CREAM
475ml/16fl oz/2 cups whipping cream
275g/10oz plain chocolate, melted
60ml/4 tbsp hazelnut-flavour liqueur

SERVES 8–10

1 In a pan large enough to hold the pears in a single layer, combine the sugar, vanilla pod and water. Bring to the boil, stirring until the sugar dissolves. Reduce the heat and add the pears. Cover and simmer for 12–15 minutes until tender. Remove from heat and leave to cool. Preheat the oven to 180°C/350°F/Gas 4.

2 Draw a 23cm/9in circle on two sheets of non-stick baking paper and place on two baking sheets.

3 Whisk the egg whites until soft peaks form then gradually add the icing sugar, whisking until stiff and glossy. Gently fold in the nuts and vanilla and spoon the meringue on to the marked circles. Bake for 1 hour. Turn off the heat and cool in the oven.

4 Slice the pear halves lengthways. Make the chocolate cream. Beat the cream to soft peaks, then fold in the melted chocolate and liqueur. Put a third of the chocolate cream into an icing bag fitted with a star tip. Spread one meringue layer with half the remaining chocolate cream and top with half the pears. Pipe rosettes around the edge.

5 Top with the second meringue and the remaining chocolate cream and pear slices. Pipe rosettes around the edge. Drizzle the melted chocolate over the pears and decorate with the chocolate caraque. Chill for 1 hour before serving.

Iced Praline Torte

INGREDIENTS

115g / 4oz / 1 cup blanched almonds
120ml / 4fl oz / ½ cup water
350g / 12oz / 1½ cups caster sugar
115g / 4oz / ⅔ cup raisins
90ml / 6 tbsp rum or brandy
115g / 4oz dark chocolate, broken into squares
30ml / 2 tbsp milk
475ml / 16fl oz / 2 cups double cream
30ml / 2 tbsp strong black coffee
16 sponge fingers
DECORATION
150ml / ¼ pint / ⅔ cup double cream
50g / 2oz / ½ cup flaked almonds, toasted
15g / ½ oz dark chocolate, melted

SERVES 8

3 Whip the double cream in a large mixing bowl until soft peaks form, then whisk in the chocolate. Fold in the praline and the soaked raisins, with any liquid.

4 Mix the coffee and the remaining rum or brandy in a shallow dish. Dip half the sponge fingers, one at a time, in the mixture, and arrange them in a layer over the bottom of the tin.

1 Lightly grease a 1.2 litre/2 pint/5 cup loaf tin. Line with greaseproof paper or non-stick baking paper. Using the almonds, water and sugar, make and grind the praline, as for Praline Ice Cream. Tip the praline into a large mixing bowl and set aside.

2 Soak the raisins in half the rum or brandy for at least 1 hour. Melt the chocolate with the milk in a heatproof bowl over a pan of barely simmering water. Allow to cool.

5 Cover with the chocolate mixture, then add another layer of dipped soaked sponge fingers. Cover the torte and freeze overnight.

6 Turn the frozen torte out on to a serving plate. Carefully remove the lining paper. Cover with the whipped cream, sprinkle the toasted almonds on top and drizzle the melted chocolate over. Serve in slices.

70

White Chocolate & Strawberry Gâteau

INGREDIENTS

115g/4oz fine quality white chocolate, chopped
120ml/4fl oz/½ cup double cream
120ml/4fl oz/½ cup milk
15ml/1 tbsp rum or vanilla essence
115g/4oz/½ cup unsalted butter, softened
175g/6oz/¾ cup caster sugar
3 eggs
225g/8oz/2 cups plain flour
5ml/1 tsp baking powder
pinch of salt
675g/1½lb/6 cups strawberries, sliced,
plus extra for decorating
750ml/1¼ pints/3 cups whipping cream
30ml/2 tbsp rum
WHITE CHOCOLATE MOUSSE FILLING
250g/9oz fine quality white chocolate, chopped
350ml/12fl oz/1½ cups whipping or
double cream
30ml/2 tbsp rum

SERVES 10

1 Preheat the oven to 180°C/350°F/Gas 4. Grease and flour two 23cm/9in round cake tins, about 5cm/2in deep. Base-line the tins with non-stick baking paper. Melt the chocolate in the cream in a double boiler over low heat, stirring until smooth. Stir in the milk and rum or vanilla essence. Set aside to cool.

2 Cream the butter and sugar until fluffy. Beat in the eggs one at a time. Sift together the flour, baking powder and salt and add to the egg mixture in batches, alternately with the melted chocolate, until just blended.

3 Divide the mixture between the prepared tins. Bake for 20–25 minutes or until a skewer inserted in the centre of each cake layer comes out clean. Cool in the tins for 10 minutes, then turn out on to wire racks, peel off the baking paper and leave to cool completely.

4 Make the filling. Melt the chocolate with the cream in a saucepan over low heat, stirring frequently. Stir in the rum and pour into a bowl. Chill until just set, then whip the mixture lightly until it has a mousse-like consistency.

5 Slice each cake layer in half horizontally to make four layers. Spread a third of the mousse on top of one layer and arrange a third of the strawberries over the mousse. Place another cake layer on top of the first and cover with mousse and strawberries as before. Repeat this process once more, then top with the final cake layer.

6 Whip the cream with the rum. Spread about half the flavoured cream over the top and sides of the cake. Use the remaining cream and strawberries to decorate the cake as desired.

Luxury Mocha Mousse

INGREDIENTS

225g/8oz fine quality plain chocolate, chopped
60ml/4 tbsp espresso or strong coffee
25g/1oz/2 tbsp butter, cut into pieces
30ml/2 tbsp brandy or rum
3 eggs, separated
pinch of salt
40g/1½oz/3 tbsp caster sugar
120ml/4fl oz/½ cup whipping cream
30ml/2 tbsp coffee-flavour liqueur
chocolate coffee beans, to decorate (optional)

SERVES 6

74

1 In a saucepan over a medium heat, melt the plain chocolate in the coffee, stirring frequently until smooth. Remove from the heat and beat in the butter and brandy or rum.

2 In a small bowl, beat the egg yolks lightly, then whisk in the melted chocolate; the mixture will thicken. Set aside to cool. In a large bowl, beat the egg whites  with an electric mixer to "break" them. Add a pinch of salt and beat on a medium speed until soft peaks form. Increase the speed and beat until stiff peaks form. Beat in the sugar, 15ml/1 tbsp at a time, beating well after each addition until the egg whites are glossy and stiff, but not dry.

3 Mix a large spoonful of whites into the chocolate mixture to lighten it, then fold the chocolate into the remaining whites. Pour into 6 individual dishes or a large glass serving bowl and chill for at least 3–4 hours, until set, before serving.

4 In a medium bowl, beat the cream and coffee-flavour liqueur until soft peaks form. Spoon into an icing bag fitted with a medium star tip and pipe rosettes or shells on to the surface of the mousse. Decorate with chocolate coffee beans, if liked.

Chocolate Cheesecake Pie

INGREDIENTS

350g/12oz/1½ cups cream cheese, softened
60ml/4 tbsp double cream
225g/8oz/1 cup caster sugar
50g/2oz/½ cup cocoa powder
2.5ml/½ tsp ground cinnamon
3 eggs
BASE
75g/3oz sweetmeal biscuits, crushed
45g/1½oz amaretti (or extra sweetmeal biscuits), crushed
75g/3oz/⅓ cup unsalted butter, melted
DECORATION
whipped cream
chocolate curls

SERVES 8

1 Preheat the oven to 180°C/350°F/Gas 4. Make the base by mixing the crushed biscuits with the melted butter. Press the mixture evenly over the bottom and sides of a 23cm/9in pie dish. Bake for 8 minutes, then cool. Leave the oven on, and put a baking sheet inside to heat.

2 Beat the cheese and cream in a bowl with an electric mixer until smooth. Beat in the sugar, cocoa and cinnamon until blended, then add the eggs, one at a time, beating for just long enough to combine. Pour the filling into the biscuit case and bake on the hot baking sheet for 25–30 minutes. The filling will sink as the cheesecake cools. Decorate with whipped cream and chocolate curls when cold.

Chocolate Fudge Gâteau

INGREDIENTS

225g/8oz plain chocolate, chopped
115g/4oz/½ cup unsalted butter, diced
150ml/¼ pint/⅔ cup water
225g/8oz/1 cup caster sugar
10ml/2 tsp vanilla essence
2 eggs, separated
150ml/¼ pint/⅔ cup soured cream
275g/10oz/2½ cups plain flour
10ml/2 tsp baking powder
5ml/1 tsp bicarbonate of soda
pinch of cream of tartar
chocolate curls, raspberries and icing sugar,
to decorate
CHOCOLATE FUDGE FILLING
450g/1lb plain chocolate, chopped
225g/8oz/1 cup unsalted butter
75ml/5 tbsp brandy
225g/8oz/¾ cup seedless raspberry preserve
GANACHE
250ml/8fl oz/1 cup double cream
225g/8oz plain chocolate, chopped
30ml/2 tbsp brandy

SERVES 18–20

1 Preheat the oven to 180°C/350°F/Gas 4. Base-line and grease a 25cm/10in springform cake tin. Place the chocolate, butter and water in a saucepan. Heat gently, until melted.

2 Pour into a large bowl and beat in the sugar and vanilla essence. Leave to cool, then beat in the egg yolks. Fold in the soured cream. Sift the dry ingredients then fold them into the mixture. Whisk the egg whites in a bowl until stiff and gently fold in.

3 Pour the mixture into the prepared tin. Bake for 45–50 minutes. Leave to cool for 10 minutes then remove from the tin, place on a wire rack and leave to cool completely. Wash and dry the tin.

4 Make the fudge filling. Gently melt the chocolate and butter with 60ml/4 tbsp of brandy. Set aside to cool. Meanwhile, cut the cake into three layers. Heat the preserve with the remaining brandy and spread over each cake layer. Leave to set.

5 Return the bottom layer to the tin, spread with half the filling, top with the middle cake layer and spread over the remaining filling. Add the top cake layer and press down gently. Chill overnight.

6 Make the ganache. Bring the cream to the boil, remove from the heat and stir in the chocolate, then the brandy. Strain, then set aside for 5 minutes to thicken. Remove the cake from its tin and pour the ganache over the top, smoothing down over the sides to cover. Pipe any remaining ganache around the base of the cake using a star-shaped nozzle. When set, decorate with chocolate curls, raspberries and icing sugar. Do not chill the glazed cake.

Sorbets & Ices

If you've never made your own ice cream, now is the time to try. It isn't difficult, just follow these easy recipes. Start with firm family favourites such as classic Vanilla or Chocolate Ice Cream, then move on to contemporary variations such as Brown Bread Ice Cream, or serve a simple ice with a rich or fruity and colourful sauce. For a simple, easy-to-prepare dessert, choose a low-fat variation of ice cream and make a refreshing sorbet. Lime & Mango Sorbet in Lime Shells will make a stunning finale to any meal.

Vanilla Ice Cream

INGREDIENTS

300ml / 10fl oz / 1¼ cups double cream
1 vanilla pod or 2.5ml / ½ tsp vanilla essence
2 eggs, lightly beaten
50g / 2oz / ¼ cup caster sugar
blackberry sauce, to serve (optional)

SERVES 4

1 Pour the cream into a heavy-based saucepan. Add the vanilla pod, if using. Bring the mixture to just below boiling point. Remove the vanilla pod.

2 Place the eggs and sugar in a heat-proof bowl. Set the bowl over a pan of barely simmering water and whisk until the mixture is pale and thick. Whisking vigorously, pour in the cream in a steady stream. Continue to whisk the mixture just until it begins to thicken.

3 Whisk in the vanilla essence, if using. Cool, then spoon into a suitable container for freezing. Freeze until crystals form around the edges, whisk until smooth, then freeze again.

4 Repeat the process once or twice, then freeze the mixture until firm. Alternatively, use an ice cream maker, following the manufacturer's instructions. Allow the ice cream to soften slightly before serving in scoops, with a fruit sauce, if liked.

VARIATION

Make a less rich version of the ice cream by substituting buttermilk for three-quarters of the double cream, and using 30ml/2 tbsp clear honey instead of the sugar.

80

Chocolate Ice Cream

INGREDIENTS

225g / 8oz plain chocolate, broken into squares
750ml / 1¼ pints / 3 cups milk
1 vanilla pod
4 egg yolks
115g / 4oz / ½ cup granulated sugar

SERVES 4–6

1 Half fill a saucepan with water, allow to boil, then remove from the heat. Place the chocolate in a heatproof bowl over the pan. Set aside until the chocolate has melted, stirring occasionally.

2 Pour the milk into a heavy-based saucepan. Add the vanilla pod. Keeping the heat fairly low, bring the mixture to just below boiling point. Remove the vanilla pod.

3 Place the egg yolks in a large heatproof bowl and whisk in the sugar. Whisk in the hot milk, then add the melted chocolate. Place the bowl over a  pan of barely simmering water and stir until the chocolate custard thickens slightly. Allow to cool.

4 Spoon the mixture into a suitable container for freezing. Freeze until ice crystals form around the edges of the container, then process or beat the mixture  until smooth. Repeat the process once or twice, then freeze the mixture until firm. Alternatively, use an ice cream maker, following the manufacturer's instructions. Allow the ice cream to soften slightly before serving it in scoops.

Rhubarb & Orange Water-ice

INGREDIENTS

*350g / 12oz pink rhubarb
grated rind and juice of 1 medium orange
30ml / 2 tbsp clear honey
5ml / 1 tsp powdered gelatine
quartered orange slices, to decorate*

SERVES 4

1 Trim the rhubarb and slice it into 2.5cm/1in lengths. If you have not been able to obtain pink (forced) rhubarb, and the stems are a bit stringy, peel them thinly before slicing.

2 Put the rhubarb into a saucepan and add half the orange rind and juice. Bring to simmering point and cook over a very low heat until the rhubarb is just tender. Stir in the honey.

3 Heat the remaining orange juice, then remove from the heat. Stir in the gelatine until it has completely dissolved, then stir the liquid into the rhubarb, and add the remaining orange rind.

4 Tip the mixture into a suitable container for freezing. Freeze until ice crystals form around the edges and the mixture is slushy.

5 Scrape the mixture into a bowl and beat until smooth. Return it to the freezer and freeze until firm. Allow the water-ice to soften slightly before serving it in scoops, decorated with quartered orange slices.

COOK'S TIP
*Pink (forced) rhubarb is naturally quite sweet,
but you may find it necessary to add a little more
honey — or caster sugar — to the mixture.*

Fresh Orange Granita

INGREDIENTS

4 large oranges
1 large lemon
150g/5oz/¾ cup granulated sugar
475ml/16 fl oz/2 cups water
blanched pared strips of orange and lemon rind,
to decorate
amaretti biscuits, to serve

SERVES 6

84

1 Thinly pare the rind from the oranges and the lemon, taking care to avoid the bitter white pith. Use a vegetable peeler for best results. Set a few pieces aside for decoration. Cut the fruit into segments and squeeze the juice into a jug. Set aside.

2 Heat the sugar and water in a heavy-based saucepan, stirring over a gentle heat until the sugar has dissolved. Bring the mixture to the boil, then boil without stirring for about 10 minutes until a syrup forms. Do not allow the syrup to burn on the saucepan bottom.

3 Remove the syrup from the heat. Then add the orange and lemon rind and shake the pan. Cover and allow the syrup to cool. The rind will infuse the syrup.

4 Strain the sugar syrup into a shallow freezer container and add the fruit juice. Stir well to mix, then freeze, uncovered, for about 4 hours or until slushy.

5 Mix the ice with a fork. Then freeze until it sets hard – about 4 hours. To serve, leave at room temperature for 10 minutes, then break up with a fork and pile into long-stemmed glasses. Decorate with strips of rind and serve with amaretti biscuits.

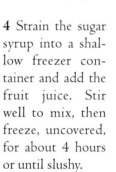

Hazelnut Ice Cream

INGREDIENTS

75g / 3oz / ¾ cup hazelnuts
75g / 3oz / 6 tbsp granulated sugar
475ml / 16fl oz / 2 cups milk
1 vanilla pod
4 egg yolks

SERVES 4–6

86

1 Spread the hazelnuts on a baking sheet. Place under a medium grill for about 5 minutes, shaking the sheet often, until the nuts are toasted. Allow them to cool slightly, then rub off the outer skins with a clean dish towel. Chop very finely or grind in a food processor or nut mill, with 30ml/2 tbsp of the sugar.

2 Pour the milk into a heavy-based saucepan. Add the vanilla pod and bring the mixture to just below boiling point. Remove the vanilla pod.

3 Place the egg yolks in a heatproof bowl. Whisk in the remaining sugar, then the hot milk. Place the bowl over a pan of barely simmering water and stir in the ground hazelnuts. Stir until the custard thickens slightly, then allow to cool.

4 Spoon the mixture into a suitable container for freezing. Freeze until ice crystals form around the edges, then process or beat the mixture until smooth. Repeat  the process twice, then freeze until the mixture is firm. Alternatively, use an ice cream maker, following the manufacturer's instructions. Allow the ice cream to soften slightly before serving it in scoops.

Brown Bread Ice Cream

INGREDIENTS

50g/2oz/½ cup hazelnuts, toasted and ground
(see Hazelnut Ice Cream)
75g/3oz/1½ cups fresh wholemeal breadcrumbs
50g/2oz/⅓ cup demerara sugar
3 egg whites
115g/4oz/½ cup caster sugar
300ml/½ pint/1¼ cups double cream
few drops of vanilla essence
fresh mint sprigs, to decorate
SAUCE
225g/8oz/1½ cups blackcurrants, thawed
if frozen
75g/3oz/6 tbsp caster sugar
15ml/1 tbsp crème de cassis

SERVES 6

1 Spread out the ground hazelnuts and breadcrumbs on a baking sheet. Sprinkle over the demerara sugar. Grill the hazelnuts under a medium heat until the mixture is crisp and browned. Leave to cool.

2 Whisk the egg whites in a grease-free bowl until stiff peaks form, then gradually whisk in the sugar until thick and glossy. Whip the cream to soft peaks; fold it into the meringue with the breadcrumb mixture and vanilla essence. Spoon the mixture into a 1.2 litre/2 pint/5 cup loaf tin. Level the surface, then cover and freeze until firm.

3 Meanwhile make the sauce. Put the blackcurrants in a bowl with the sugar. Toss gently, cover and leave for 30 minutes, then purée in a blender or food processor. Press through a nylon sieve into a bowl, stir in the crème de cassis and chill well. Serve the ice cream in slices, with the sauce. Decorate with the fresh mint sprigs.

Turkish Delight Ice Cream

INGREDIENTS

300ml / ½ pint / 1¼ cups milk
4 egg yolks
115g / 4oz / ½ cup caster sugar
175g / 6oz / 1 cup rose-flavoured Turkish delight, chopped
30–45ml / 2–3 tbsp water
15ml / 1 tbsp rosewater
300ml / ½ pint / 1¼ cups double cream
thin almond biscuits, to serve (optional)

SERVES 6

1 Bring the milk to the boil in a large heavy-based pan. Whisk the egg yolks with the caster sugar in a heatproof bowl. Then whisk in the hot milk.

2 Place the bowl over a pan of barely simmering water and stir until the custard thickens slightly. Remove from the heat, cover the surface of the custard closely with greaseproof paper (to prevent the formation of a skin) and allow to cool.

3 Meanwhile, heat the Turkish delight and water in a small pan. When most of the mixture has melted, and only a few lumps remain, stir it into the cold custard, with the rosewater and cream.

4 Spoon the mixture into a suitable container for freezing. Freeze until ice crystals form around the edges, then tip into a bowl and whisk the mixture well.

Return to the freezer container. Repeat the process once or twice, then freeze until firm. Alternatively, use an ice cream maker, following the manufacturer's instructions. Allow the ice cream to soften slightly before serving it in small scoops with the thin almond biscuits, if using.

COOK'S TIP
This ice cream will look extra special decorated with a scattering of pink rose petals, if you have any.

Coconut Ice Cream

INGREDIENTS

400g/14oz can evaporated milk
400g/14oz can condensed milk
400g/14oz can coconut milk
5ml/1 tsp grated nutmeg
5ml/1 tsp almond essence
lemon balm sprigs, lime slices and shredded coconut, to decorate

SERVES 8

1 Mix the evaporated milk, condensed milk and coconut milk in a large bowl which will fit in the freezer. Stir in the nutmeg and almond essence.

2 Freeze until ice crystals begin to form around the edges of the mixture, then remove from the freezer and whisk by hand or with a hand-held mixer until the mixture is fluffy and has almost doubled in bulk.

3 Tip the mixture into a suitable container for freezing, cover and freeze until solid. Allow the ice cream to soften slightly before serving in scoops, decorated with lemon balm sprigs, lime slices and the shredded coconut.

Kulfi

Ingredients

3 x 400ml/14fl oz cans evaporated milk
3 egg whites
350g/12oz/2⅔ cups icing sugar
5ml/1 tsp ground cardamom
15ml/1 tbsp rosewater
175g/6oz/1½ cups pistachio nuts, chopped
75g/3oz/¾ cup flaked almonds
75g/3oz/½ cup sultanas
25g/1oz/3 tbsp glacé cherries, halved

Serves 4–6

1 Remove the labels from the cans of evaporated milk and lay them on their sides in a saucepan with a tight-fitting lid. Pour in water to come three-quarters of the way up the cans. Bring to the boil, lower the heat, cover and simmer for 20 minutes. Let the unopened cans cool in the water, then remove and place in the fridge for 24 hours.

2 Whisk the egg whites in a grease-free bowl until stiff peaks form. Open the cans and pour the milk into a chilled bowl. Whisk until doubled in bulk, then fold in the egg whites and icing sugar.

3 Gently fold in the ground cardamom, rosewater, nuts, sultanas and cherries. Cover the bowl and freeze until ice crystals form around the edges, then mix

well with a fork. Return to the freezer and freeze again until firm. Allow the kulfi to soften slightly before serving it in scoops.

91

Mint Ice Cream

INGREDIENTS

600ml/1 pint/2½ cups single cream
1 vanilla pod or 2.5ml/½ tsp vanilla essence
8 egg yolks
75g/3oz/6 tbsp caster sugar
60ml/4 tbsp finely chopped fresh mint
fresh mint sprigs, to decorate

SERVES 8

92

1 Pour the cream into a heavy-based saucepan. Add the vanilla pod, if using. Keeping the heat fairly low, bring the mixture to just below boiling point. Remove the vanilla pod.

2 Place the egg yolks and sugar in a large mixing bowl. Beat until the mixture is pale and light, using a balloon whisk or an electric beater. Transfer to a pan.

3 Whisking vigorously, pour the hot cream into the saucepan in a steady stream. Continue to whisk until the mixture thickens slightly. Whisk in the vanilla essence, if using. Leave to cool.

4 Stir in the mint. Spoon the mixture into a suitable container for freezing. Freeze until ice crystals form around the edges, then beat the mixture until smooth.

5 Repeat the process once or twice, then freeze until firm. Alternatively, use an ice cream maker, following the manufacturer's instructions. Allow the ice cream to stand at room temperature for 15 minutes before serving, to soften slightly. This ice cream looks spectacular scooped into an ice bowl, decorated with the fresh mint sprigs.

Rocky Road Ice Cream

INGREDIENTS

115g/4oz plain chocolate, broken into squares
150ml/¼ pint/⅔ cup milk
300ml/½ pint/1¼ cups double cream
115g/4oz/1½ cups marshmallows,
chopped if large
50g/2oz/½ cup glacé cherries, chopped
50g/2oz/½ cup crumbled shortbread biscuits
30ml/2 tbsp chopped walnuts

SERVES 6

2 Whip the cream in a bowl until it just holds its shape. Beat in the chocolate milk, then tip the mixture into a suitable container for freezing. Freeze until ice crystals form around the edges. Alternatively, churn the mixture in an ice cream maker until it is thick and almost frozen.

3 Using a spatula, stir the marshmallows, chopped glacé cherries, crumbled biscuits and walnuts into the iced mixture. Freeze again until it is firm. Allow the ice cream to soften slightly before serving it in scoops or slices.

94

1 Melt the squares of chocolate in the milk in a large saucepan over a gentle heat, stirring from time to time. Allow the chocolate milk to cool completely.

COOK'S TIP
Use kitchen scissors to chop the marshmallows, dipping the blades in a jug of boiling water between snips.

Coffee Ice Cream with Caramelized Pecans

INGREDIENTS

300ml/½ pint/1¼ cups milk
15ml/1 tbsp demerara sugar
15ml/1 tbsp instant coffee granules
1 egg, plus 2 yolks
300ml/½ pint/1¼ cups double cream
15ml/1 tbsp caster sugar
CARAMELIZED PECANS
115g/4oz/1 cup pecan nut halves
50g/2oz/⅓ cup soft dark brown sugar
30ml/2 tbsp water

SERVES 4–6

1 Heat the milk and demerara sugar in a heavy-based saucepan, stirring until the sugar dissolves. Bring to the boil, remove from the heat and stir in the instant coffee until dissolved.

2 Combine the egg and extra yolks in a heatproof bowl. Set the bowl over a saucepan of barely simmering water and whisk until the eggs are pale and thick. Remove from the heat.

3 Whisking vigorously, pour in the coffee-flavoured milk in a steady stream. Replace over the water and stir until the custard thickens slightly. Leave the mixture to cool.

4 Whip the cream with the caster sugar until soft peaks form. Fold it into the coffee custard, then tip the mixture into a suitable container for freezing. Freeze until ice crystals form around the edges, then beat the mixture until smooth. Repeat the process once or twice, then freeze until firm. Alternatively, use an ice cream maker, following the manufacturer's instructions.

5 Caramelize the pecans. Preheat the oven to 180°C/350°F/Gas 4. Spread the nuts in a single layer on a baking sheet. Bake for 10–15 minutes, checking frequently, until they are roasted.

6 Next, dissolve the brown sugar in the water over a low heat, then bring to the boil. When the mixture bubbles and begins to turn golden, tip in the  roasted pecans. Cook for 1–2 minutes over a medium heat until the pecans are well coated.

7 Spread the pecan nuts on a lightly oiled baking sheet and set aside until they have cooled. Allow the ice cream to soften slightly at room temperature before serving it in scoops, with the caramelized pecans.

Summer Fruit Salad Ice Cream

INGREDIENTS

*900g / 2lb / 5 cups mixed soft summer fruit
(such as raspberries, strawberries,
blackcurrants, redcurrants)
175ml / 6fl oz / ¾ cup red grape juice
15ml / 1 tbsp powdered gelatine
2 eggs, separated
250ml / 8fl oz / 1 cup natural yogurt*

SERVES 6

98

1 Set half the fruit aside for the decoration. Purée the rest in a blender or food processor, then rub through a sieve into a bowl, to remove any seeds.

2 Heat the grape juice in a small pan until just below boiling point. Remove from the heat and sprinkle the gelatine over the surface. Stir the grape juice to

dissolve the gelatine completely. Cool slightly.

3 Whisk the egg yolks, yogurt and dissolved gelatine into the fruit purée. Pour into a suitable container for freezing. Freeze until crystals form around the edges and the mixture is slushy.

4 Whisk the egg whites in a grease-free bowl until stiff peaks form. Tip the half-frozen yogurt ice cream into a bowl and quickly fold in the egg whites.

5 Return the mixture to the freezer container and freeze until solid. Soften slightly before serving in scoops, with the reserved soft fruits.

COOK'S TIP

Hull the fruit used for the purée, but leave the rest whole — attached to the stalks — for the decoration.

Mango Sorbet with Mango Sauce

INGREDIENTS

2 x 400g / 14oz cans sliced mangoes, drained
2.5ml / ½ tsp lemon juice
grated rind of 1 orange and 1 lemon
4 egg whites
50g / 2oz / ¼ cup caster sugar
120ml / 4fl oz / ½ cup double cream
50g / 2oz / ½ cup icing sugar

SERVES 4–6

100

1 Purée the mangoes in a blender or food processor. Tip half the purée into a large bowl which will fit in the freezer. Stir in the lemon juice and citrus rind. Reserve the remaining purée for the sauce.

2 Whisk the egg whites in a grease-free bowl until stiff peaks form, then gradually whisk in the caster sugar until thick and glossy. Fold into the mango purée and freeze until ice crystals form around the edges of the bowl.

3 Beat the mixture until it is smooth, then scrape into a freezer container and freeze until firm.

4 Make the mango sauce. Whip the double cream with the icing sugar until soft peaks form, then fold in the reserved mango purée. Spoon into a serving bowl, then cover the bowl and chill for 24 hours.

5 Allow the sorbet to soften for about 10 minutes before serving in scoops, topped with the sauce.

Watermelon Sorbet

INGREDIENTS

1kg / 2¼lb piece of watermelon
225g / 8oz / 1 cup caster sugar
juice of 1 lemon
120ml / 4fl oz / ½ cup water
2 egg whites
fresh mint leaves, to decorate

SERVES 6

1 Cut the watermelon into cubes, discarding the peel and any seeds. Mash a quarter of the cubes in a shallow bowl. Purée the remaining watermelon in a blender or food processor, in batches if necessary.

2 Mix the sugar, lemon juice and water in a saucepan. Stir over a low heat until the sugar dissolves, then boil, without stirring, for 2 minutes. Tip into a large bowl and stir in the watermelon purée and the mashed watermelon. Cool, then pour the mixture into a suitable container for freezing.

3 Freeze until ice crystals form around the edges of the mixture, then scrape it into a bowl and beat until smooth. Freeze the mixture as before, then beat and freeze again.

4 In a grease-free bowl, whisk the egg whites until they form soft peaks. Beat the iced mixture again, then fold in the egg whites. Return the sorbet to the freezer container, freeze for 1 hour, then beat again and freeze until firm. Allow the sorbet to soften before serving in scoops, decorated with the fresh mint leaves.

Chocolate Sorbet with Red Fruits

INGREDIENTS

475ml/16fl oz/2 cups water
45ml/3 tbsp clear honey
115g/4oz/½ cup caster sugar
75g/3oz/¾ cup cocoa powder
50g/2oz plain chocolate, broken into squares
400g/14oz/3 cups soft red fruits (such as
raspberries, strawberries, redcurrants), to serve

SERVES 6

102

2 Remove the saucepan from the heat, add the chocolate, a few squares at a time, and stir until melted. Set the saucepan aside until the mixture has cooled.

3 For a really fine texture, churn the mixture in an ice cream maker until it has completely frozen. Alternatively, pour the mixture into a container suitable

for use in the freezer, freeze until slushy, then whisk until smooth and freeze again. Whisk for a second time before the mixture hardens completely.

4 Allow the sorbet to soften slightly at room temperature before serving in scoops or ovals, decorated with the soft berry fruits.

1 Mix the water, honey and caster sugar in a large saucepan. Gradually add the cocoa powder, and stir continuously until the liquid is smooth. Cook

gently over a low heat, stirring occasionally, until the sugar and cocoa have dissolved completely.

COOK'S TIP

To shape the sorbet into ovals, use two tablespoons. Scoop out the sorbet with one tablespoon, then use the other to smooth it off and transfer it to a plate.

Blackcurrant Sorbet

INGREDIENTS

500g / 1¼lb blackcurrants
115g / 4oz / ½ cup caster sugar
120ml / 4fl oz / ½ cup water
15ml / 1 tbsp egg white
fresh mint sprigs, to decorate

SERVES 4

104

1 Strip the blackcurrants from their stalks by pulling them through the tines of a fork. Mix the sugar and water in a saucepan. Stir over a low heat until the sugar dissolves, then boil, without stirring, for 2 minutes.

2 Purée the blackcurrants with the lemon juice in a blender or food processor. Add the sugar syrup and process briefly to mix. Press the mixture through a sieve set over a bowl, to remove any seeds.

3 Pour the blackcurrant purée into a non-metallic container suitable for use in the freezer. Cover and freeze until ice crystals form around the edges and the mixture is slushy.

4 Scrape spoonfuls of sorbet into a blender or food processor. Process until smooth, then, with the motor running, add the egg white and process until well mixed.

5 Tip the sorbet back into the freezer container and freeze until almost firm. Process again. Serve immediately or return to the freezer until solid, in which case the sorbet should be allowed to soften slightly before serving. Serve in scoops, decorated with the fresh mint sprigs.

Lime & Mango Sorbet in Lime Shells

INGREDIENTS

4 large limes
7.5ml / 1½ tsp powdered gelatine
1 ripe mango, peeled and chopped
2 egg whites
15ml / 1 tbsp caster sugar
pared lime rind strips, to decorate

SERVES 4

1 Slice the tops off the limes, and take a slim slice off the bottom of each so that they stand upright. Carefully scoop the flesh into a bowl, keeping the lime shells intact. Squeeze out all the juice from the lime flesh and put 45ml/3 tbsp of it in a small heatproof bowl. Sprinkle the gelatine on top and leave until spongy.

2 Purée the mango with the remaining lime juice (about 30ml/2 tbsp) in a blender or food processor. Place the heatproof bowl over a small pan of hot water and stir until the gelatine has dissolved completely. Add it to the mango purée and process briefly to mix.

3 Whisk the egg whites in a grease-free bowl until they form soft peaks. Whisk in the caster sugar, then fold into the mango mixture. Spoon into the lime shells, mounding the mixture. Freeze any excess sorbet in ramekin dishes.

4 Freeze the filled shells until firm, wrap them in clear film and replace them in the freezer. Before serving, unwrap the limes and allow the sorbet to soften slightly. Decorate with the lime rind strips.

Specialities

Think of the heat of summer and the ideal dessert that springs to mind is always something cool and refreshing. This connoisseur's collection of tried and tested speciality iced desserts contains something for every taste and what's more the ices are made in advance of the occasion and the components assembled quickly and easily at the last minute. For a feast of ice cream, serve glorious Black Forest Sundaes, or for a spectacular finale choose a lush and colourful layered Cranberry Bombe decorated with your choice of colourful additions.

Coffee Granita

INGREDIENTS

115g/4oz/½ cup granulated sugar
475ml/16fl oz/2 cups water
*250ml/8fl oz/1 cup very strong black
coffee, cooled*
dessert biscuits, to serve
DECORATION
*250ml/8fl oz/1 cup double cream, whipped
with 10ml/2 tsp icing sugar*

SERVES 4

108

2 Add the coffee to the sugar syrup in the saucepan and mix together. Then pour the mixture into a shallow freezer tray and freeze for several hours until it is solid.

3 To remove from the freezer tray, plunge the bottom of the container into very hot water for a few seconds, then turn out the frozen coffee mixture and chop it into large chunks.

4 Place the frozen coffee chunks in a food processor and process until the ice breaks down to a mass of small crystals. Spoon into tall serving glasses and top each glass with a spoonful of the sweetened whipped cream.

1 Mix the sugar and water in a saucepan. Stir over a low heat until the sugar dissolves, then boil, without stirring, for about 2 minutes. Remove from the heat and allow to cool.

COOK'S TIP
If you do not wish to serve the granita immediately, pour the processed mixture back into the freezer tray and freeze until serving time. Thaw for a few minutes before serving, or process again.

Praline Ice Cream in Baskets

INGREDIENTS

50g / 2oz / ½ cup blanched almonds
60ml / 4 tbsp water
175g / 6oz / ¾ cup caster sugar
475ml / 16fl oz / 2 cups milk
6 egg yolks
250ml / 8fl oz / 1 cup double cream
8 biscuit baskets, to serve

SERVES 6–8

110

1 Brush a baking sheet lightly with oil. Mix the nuts, water and 65g/ 2½oz/5 tbsp of the sugar in a saucepan. Stir over a low heat until the sugar dissolves,

then boil, without stirring, until the syrup is a medium caramel colour and the nuts begin to pop. Carefully pour the nuts on to the baking sheet and set aside until cold.

2 Break the nut praline into small pieces. Grind in a food processor until fine. Then, in a large saucepan, bring the milk to just below boiling point.

3 Whisk the egg yolks and remaining sugar in a heatproof bowl until pale and thick. Whisk in the hot milk, then place the bowl over a pan of simmering water and stir until the mixture thickens. Remove the bowl from the heat and stir in the double cream. Set aside to cool.

4 Stir the praline into the mixture, reserving 30ml/2 tbsp for decoration. Churn in an ice cream maker until frozen. Alternatively, pour it into a freezer container, freeze until slushy, whisk until smooth, then freeze again. Whisk for a second time before the mixture hardens completely.

5 Allow the ice cream to soften before serving, in the baskets, sprinkled with the reserved praline.

Black Forest Sundae

INGREDIENTS

400g/14oz can pitted black cherries in syrup
15ml/1 tbsp cornflour
45ml/3 tbsp kirsch
150ml/¼ pint/⅔ cup whipping cream
15ml/1 tbsp icing sugar
600ml/1 pint/2½ cups chocolate ice cream
115g/4oz chocolate cake, cut in large pieces
vanilla ice cream, to serve
8 fresh cherries, to decorate

SERVES 4

1 Strain the cherry syrup into a large saucepan, then spoon 30ml/2 tbsp of the syrup into a small bowl. Stir in the cornflour until the mixture is smooth.

2 Bring the syrup in the pan to the boil. Stir in the cornflour mixture, lower the heat and simmer briefly to thicken. Add the cherries, stir in the kirsch and spread the mixture out on a baking sheet to cool.

3 In a bowl, whip the cream with the icing sugar until soft peaks form. Place a spoonful of the cherry mixture in each of four sundae glasses. Top with layers of chocolate ice cream, pieces of chocolate cake, whipped cream and more cherry mixture, until the glasses are almost full.

4 Finish off each sundae with a final piece of chocolate cake, two scoops of ice cream and a whirl of fresh whipped cream. Decorate each with 2 fresh cherries and serve at once.

VARIATION

This particular sundae is based upon Black Forest Gateau, but you don't have to be tied to these ingredients. Invent your own combinations of fruit, ice cream, cake and cream.

112

Blackberry & Apple Romanoff

INGREDIENTS

4 sharp eating apples
45ml/3 tbsp caster sugar
250ml/8fl oz/1 cup whipping cream
5ml/1 tsp grated lemon rind
90ml/6 tbsp Greek-style yogurt
4–6 crisp meringues, roughly crumbled
225g/8oz/1½ cups fresh or thawed frozen blackberries
whipped cream, blackberries and fresh mint sprigs, to decorate

SERVES 6

114

2 Whip the cream with the remaining sugar in a large mixing bowl. Fold in the grated lemon rind and yogurt, then stir in the mashed apples and the meringues.

3 Gently stir in the blackberries, then tip all of the mixture into the pudding basin. Cover the basin with clear film and freeze for 1–3 hours, until the mixture is firm.

1 Line a 900ml/ 1½ pint/4 cup pudding basin with clear film. Peel and core the apples, then slice them into a heavy-based frying pan. Add 30ml/2 tbsp

of the sugar. Cook the mixture for 2–3 minutes, or until the apples soften. Mash them with a fork and set the frying pan aside to cool.

4 Turn out on to a chilled plate, lift off the clear film and pipe whipped cream around the base. Decorate with the blackberries and fresh mint sprigs.

Cranberry Bombe

INGREDIENTS

SORBET CENTRE
225g/8oz/2 cups fresh or frozen cranberries,
thawed if frozen, plus extra to decorate
150ml/¼ pint/⅔ cup orange juice
finely grated rind of ½ orange
½ tsp allspice
50g/2oz/⅓ cup raw sugar
OUTER LAYER
1 quantity Vanilla Ice Cream
1oz/2 tbsp chopped angelica
1oz/2 tbsp mixed peel
½oz/1 tbsp flaked almonds, toasted

SERVES 6

1 Line a 1.2 litre/ 2 pint/5 cup pudding basin with clear film. Make the sorbet centre. Put the cranberries, orange juice, rind and spice in a saucepan. Cook

gently until the cranberries are soft. Stir in the sugar, then purée the mixture in a food processor until almost smooth, but with some texture. Set the saucepan aside to cool.

2 Allow the Vanilla Ice Cream to soften slightly, then tip it into a bowl and stir in the chopped angelica, mixed peel and flaked almonds.

3 Pack the mixture into the prepared pudding basin and use the back of a dessert spoon to hollow out the centre. Cover and freeze until firm.

4 Fill the hollow in the ice cream with the cranberry mixture. Freeze again until firm. When ready to serve, invert the bombe on a chilled plate and

lift off the clear film. Allow the bombe to soften slightly at room temperature before serving it in slices, decorated with fresh cranberries.

COOK'S TIP
This luxurious iced dessert tastes great on hot summer evenings but it also makes a wonderful alternative to Christmas Pudding. It is easy to make, popular with children and requires absolutely no attention on the day!

Frozen Apple & Blackberry Terrine

INGREDIENTS

450g / 1lb cooking apples
300ml / ½ pint / 1¼ cups apple juice
15ml / 1 tbsp clear honey
5ml / 1 tsp vanilla essence
350g / 12oz / 2 cups fresh or thawed frozen
blackberries
15ml / 1 tbsp powdered gelatine
2 egg whites
fresh apple slices and blackberries, to decorate

SERVES 6

1 Peel, core and chop the apples. Place them in a saucepan with half the apple juice. Bring to the boil, then cover and simmer the apples gently until they are tender.

2 Purée the apples, with the honey and vanilla essence, in a blender or food processor. Spoon half the apple purée into a bowl and set it aside. Add half the blackberries to the remaining apple purée and process until smooth. Press the blackberry and apple purée through a sieve to remove the seeds.

3 Then pour the remaining apple juice into the clean pan and bring to just below boiling point. Sprinkle the gelatine over and stir until completely dissolved. Stir

half the gelatine into the plain apple purée and half into the blackberry and apple purée. Leave both purées to cool until they are on the verge of setting.

4 Whisk the egg whites until almost stiff, then fold them into the plain apple purée. Spoon half the mixture into a separate bowl. Stir in the remaining whole blackberries, then tip the mixture into a 1.75 litre/3 pint/7½ cup loaf tin, packing it down firmly. Top with the blackberry purée, spreading it level, then the remaining apple purée. Freeze the mixture until firm. Allow the terrine to soften slightly before serving it in slices, decorated with the fresh apple slices and the blackberries.

Fried Wontons & Ice Cream

INGREDIENTS

oil, for deep frying
12 wonton wrappers
8 scoops of your favourite ice cream (or
4 scoops each of two varieties)

SERVES 4

120

1 Heat the oil in a deep-fryer or large saucepan to 180°C/350°F or until a cube of dried bread browns in 30–45 seconds.

2 Add a few wonton wrappers at a time, so that they do not crowd the pan too much. Fry for 1–2 minutes on each side, until the wrappers are crisp and light golden brown. Lift out and drain on kitchen paper.

3 To serve, place one wonton on each plate. Top with a scoop of ice cream, then add a second wonton and a second scoop of ice cream. Finish with a final wonton. Serve at once.

COOK'S TIP

Mix and match the scoops of ice cream to contrast the colours but take care to choose complementary flavours. Try coffee with hazelnut, Turkish delight with vanilla or chocolate with mint.

Café Glacé

INGREDIENTS

600ml/1 pint/2½ cups water
30–45ml/2–3 tbsp instant coffee granules
15ml/1 tbsp caster sugar
600ml/1 pint/2½ cups milk
6 ice cubes
12 scoops of vanilla ice cream
6 chocolate flakes, to decorate
12 crisp dessert biscuits, to serve

SERVES 6

1 Bring 120ml/ 4floz/½ cup of the water to the boil, pour into a small bowl and stir in the coffee. Stir in the sugar until dissolved. Leave to cool, then chill for about 2 hours.

2 Mix the milk and remaining water in a large jug. Add the chilled coffee mixture and mix well. Divide the mixture among six brandy snifters or cocktail glasses, filling them three-quarters full.

3 Add an ice cube and 2 scoops of vanilla ice cream to each glass. Decorate with the chocolate flakes and serve with the biscuits.

Iced Mint & Chocolate Cooler

INGREDIENTS

60ml/4 tbsp drinking chocolate
400ml/14fl oz/1¾ cups chilled milk
150ml/¼ pint/⅔ cup natural yogurt
2.5ml/½ tsp peppermint essence
4 scoops of chocolate ice cream
mint leaves and chocolate shapes, to decorate

SERVES 4

122

2 Pour the liquid into a large mixing bowl or large jug and whisk in the remaining milk. Then, add the natural yogurt and the peppermint essence to the jug.

3 Pour the mixture into four tall glasses and top each with a scoop of chocolate ice cream. Decorate each of the glasses with the fresh mint leaves and assorted chocolate shapes. Serve immediately.

I Place the drinking chocolate in a small saucepan and stir in about 120ml/4fl oz/ ½ cup of chilled milk. Gently heat the liquid, stirring constantly, until almost boiling, then remove the saucepan from the heat and allow the liquid to cool.

COOK'S TIP
Cocoa powder can be used instead of drinking chocolate, if preferred, but remember that cocoa can be quite bitter: you may need to add sugar to taste.

Blushing Piña Colada

INGREDIENTS

1 banana
1 thick slice of pineapple
75ml / 5 tbsp pineapple juice
1 scoop strawberry ice cream or sorbet
25ml / 1½ tbsp coconut milk
1 small scoop finely crushed ice (see Cook's Tip)
30ml / 2 tbsp grenadine
stemmed maraschino cherries, to decorate

SERVES 2

124

1 Peel the banana and chop it roughly. Cut two small wedges from the pineapple and set aside for the decoration. Then peel and chop the remaining pine-

apple and add it to the blender with the banana and pineapple juice. Process to a smooth purée.

2 Add the strawberry ice cream or sorbet to the blender. Pour in the coconut milk and add the scoop of finely crushed ice. Process until smooth.

3 Then divide the drink between two large, well-chilled glasses. Trickle the grenadine syrup over the top of the piña colada; it will filter through the drink to give a pink blush effect.

4 Slit the reserved pineapple wedges, and slip one on to the rim of each glass. Then add a maraschino cherry in the same way. Serve the blushing piña colada with drinking straws.

COOK'S TIP

Never try to crush ice in a blender; it will ruin the blades. Put the ice cubes in a strong plastic bag and crush them finely with a rolling pin before adding to the blender.

Ice Cream Strawberry Shortcake

INGREDIENTS

*3 x 15cm / 6in ready-made sponge cake cases
or shortcakes
1.2 litres / 2 pints / 5 cups vanilla or
strawberry ice cream, softened until spreadable
675g / 1½lb / 5 cups hulled strawberries,
halved if large
whipped cream, to serve (optional)*

SERVES 4

1 If you are using sponge cake cases, trim off the raised edges with a sharp serrated knife. The sponge trimmings can be saved and used to make individual trifles.

2 Using two-thirds of the ice cream and hulled strawberries, sandwich the sponge cake cases or shortcakes together.

3 Spoon the remaining ice cream on top, crown with the remaining strawberries. Serve the shortcake at once, with whipped cream, if liked.

COOK'S TIP

There is no neat way of cutting this delicious dessert. It will look glorious until you actually start to serve it, and that's what really matters.

Index